DATE DUE

The Ethics of the Market

The Ethics of the Market

John Meadowcroft

Deputy Editorial Director, Institute of Economic Affairs, London
and
*Lecturer in Parliament and Politics, Hansard Scholars Programme,
London School of Economics and Political Science, London*

palgrave
macmillan

First published 2005 by
PALGRAVE MACMILLAN
Houndmills, Basingstoke, Hampshire RG21 6XS and
175 Fifth Avenue, New York, N.Y. 10010
Companies and representatives throughout the world

PALGRAVE MACMILLAN is the global academic imprint of the Palgrave Macmillan division of St. Martin's Press, LLC and of Palgrave Macmillan Ltd. Macmillan® is a registered trademark in the United States, United Kingdom and other countries. Palgrave is a registered trademark in the European Union and other countries.

ISBN-13: 978–1–4039–2104–8 hardback
ISBN-10: 1–4039–2104–0 hardback

This book is printed on paper suitable for recycling and made from fully managed and sustained forest sources.

A catalogue record for this book is available from the British Library.

Library of Congress Cataloging-in-Publication Data
Meadowcroft, John, 1971–
    The ethics of the market / John Meadowcroft.
        p.   cm.
    Includes bibliographical references and index.
    ISBN 1–4039–2104–0 (cloth)
    1. Capital market—Moral and ethical aspects. 2. Business ethics.
    I. Title.
    HG4523.M43 2005
    174′.4 —dc22   2005049334

10   9   8   7   6   5   4   3   2   1
14   13   12   11   10   09   08   07   06   05

Printed and bound in Great Britain by
Antony Rowe Ltd, Chippenham and Eastbourne

For my mother and father

Contents

Acknowledgements   ix

1 **Introduction**   1
   The *doux-commerce* thesis and beyond   5
   The market and the good   7
   The structure of the book   9

2 **Markets and Ethics**   12
   The market, self-ownership and 'exit'   14
   Prosperity, self-ownership and the market process 19
   Profits, altruism and the market   24
   Conclusion   30

3 **Prices and Needs**   33
   Prices, need and purchasing power   35
   Prices as a 'category mistake'   36
   The informational efficiency of prices   38
   Purchasing power, prices and distribution   42
   Prices and values   44
   Prices, information and coordination   48
   Conclusion   52

4 **Distribution and Justice**   55
   Justice, distribution and entitlement   57
   Value, desert and the market process   67
   The difference principle and the benefits of
     inequality   70
   Inequality, economic mobility and equality
     of opportunity   77
   Poverty, sufficiency and a guaranteed minimum
     income   80
   Conclusion   85

5   **Exploitation and Coercion**   **88**
    The exploitative, coercive marketplace   90
    Marxist theories of power and exploitation   92
    Asymmetries of bargaining power and exploitation   93
    Coercion and choice: 'your money or your life'   95
    Choice and constraint in the marketplace   98
    Monopsony or market?   100
    The surplus and the role of the entrepreneur   105
    Conclusion   107
    Note   108

6   **Culture and Well-being**   **109**
    Choice and the citizen-consumer dichotomy   110
    Consumerism and the 'hedonic treadmill'   114
    Choice and well-being in the marketplace   117
    Growth, prosperity and well-being   120
    Culture in the marketplace   124
    Conclusion   128
    Notes   129

7   **Morality and Commerce**   **131**
    The 'self-devouring' market economy   133
    The erosion of traditional values and institutions   134
    Self-interest, subjectivism and the market   138
    The market, firms and friendship   140
    Incentives, probity and self-regulation   142
    The market and civil society   147
    Markets, choice and morals   150
    Conclusion   154

8   **Conclusion**   **155**

Bibliography   159

Index   169

Acknowledgements

I would like to thank a number of friends and colleagues who read and commented upon an earlier version of this book (or a part of the book): Dr Niclas Berggren of the Ratio Institute, Stockholm; Dr Adrian Blau of Manchester University; Professor Philip Booth of the Institute of Economic Affairs and Cass Business School; Dr Mark Pennington of Queen Mary, University of London. I would also like to thank the publisher's two anonymous referees for their comments that contributed to the development of the book. The usual caveat applies. I would also like to put on record my gratitude to three people who have had a huge positive impact on my professional life: Simon Hughes MP, Professor Nirmala Rao and Professor Philip Booth. Finally, this book is dedicated to my mother and father for all their love, support and encouragement.

John Meadowcroft

1
Introduction

After the collapse of Communism in Eastern Europe and the former Soviet Union and the 'rolling back of the state' in liberal democracies across the world in the final two decades of the twentieth century it is now widely held that the central intellectual debate in political economy has shifted from the question of whether capitalism or socialism is the most efficacious economic system to the question of how the state should manage and regulate a market economy. According to Keat (1993, p. 6), 'Now that the political and theoretical contest between market and state seems largely settled to the former's advantage', the intellectual focus has shifted to 'some important issues about the nature and place of economic markets', and, in particular, 'the boundaries [that] should be drawn around the domain of activities to be governed by the market'.

It is argued that we no longer face a choice between two competing economic systems, but a choice between different regimes for the regulation of a market economy, ranging from an essentially free, self-regulating market where few areas of social and economic life are not exposed to market forces, to a heavily regulated market where market forces only operate freely in specific, demarcated spheres, such as in the production of consumer goods. In the words of John Gray (1993, p. 122) in his book *Beyond the New Right*:

> The real space for public discourse is not between the two extremes, but in the area of detailed debate about the scope and content of public goods, the depth and limits of the common

culture, the relative costs of government failure and market failure, and the content and levels of provision of basic needs. This is the agenda of policy that should inform public discourse henceforth, and upon which political consensus in Britain and other similar countries should in future be established.

In the wake of the political, social and economic changes of the last quarter of the twentieth century, the political economy of the future is said to concern questions of expediency rather than of principle. Rather than a choice between the philosophical 'extremes' of market liberalism and state socialism, now the challenge is said to be the construction of a regulatory regime that imposes limits on the operation of markets necessary to preserve the social and moral fabric of society and ensure adequate provision of public goods without sacrificing the benefits of efficiency and prosperity that only a market economy can achieve.

On the face of it, it would appear that the capitalist economic model has emerged triumphant from the twentieth century and the only point of contention is the appropriate role of the state in regulating a vibrant and dominant market sector. While it is undoubtedly true that the state socialist alternative to capitalism has withered away, it is nevertheless the case that many of the regulatory measures implemented in contemporary liberal democracies impose equal if not greater restrictions on economic freedom and individual liberty than the direct interventions that were undertaken during the post-war consensus.

Whereas in the past the state took direct control of the 'commanding heights' of the economy via nationalization, today the state regulates the privately owned utilities to set prices and limit profits. In this and in all other sectors of the economy the state may intervene to prevent mergers and takeovers in order to preserve the 'competitive' structure of the economy and may prosecute those private companies whose businesses practices are deemed to be 'anti-competitive'. If successful, such a prosecution can mean the breaking-up of the company against the wishes of its owners.

Whereas in the past the state directly determined the incomes of large sections of the workforce via corporatist wage negotiations, now the state imposes a minimum wage on the whole economy that prevents employers from freely deciding how much to pay their employees.

Whereas in the past the state directly provided 'social housing' for people on low incomes, today the government uses land-use planning regulations to force private sector developers to build 'affordable housing' and in some places has imposed restrictions as to whom private homeowners may sell their properties to in order to ensure that certain categories of people can afford to purchase properties where demand is high.

Furthermore, in many areas, such as education and healthcare, the role of the state as the principal direct provider of services continues unchanged.

Overall, the state remains the dominant economic actor in contemporary liberal democracies, consuming, for example, more than thirty per cent of GDP in the United States and more than forty per cent in the UK. While many have heralded the victory of the market over the state, in reality the desire to constrain the operation of the market has never gone away, it has simply taken on new forms, which though more subtle are no less intrusive. It is not the case that such regulation is neutral: it imposes economic costs and has a direct impact on people's freedom to live their lives as they choose.

Moral arguments against the market

Among the most important justifications for such intervention and external regulation of the market are moral and ethical. It is widely argued, for example by Cohen (1995), Galbraith (2002) and Miller (2001), that because the market produces acute economic inequalities the distribution of income and wealth cannot be left to market forces; social justice demands that the most extreme economic inequalities be mediated by the intervention of government. According to Galbraith (2002), without state intervention the inequalities produced by the unfettered operation of market forces will create dysfunctional and unstable societies characterized by high levels of crime and unemployment. It is on these grounds that progressive and redistributive income tax, capital gains tax, inheritance tax, stamp duty, corporation tax, special taxes on 'windfall profits' and many more equalizing measures are justified and implemented within contemporary liberal democracies.

It is also widely contended that the state should intervene in labour markets to prohibit or 'block' transactions that are deemed exploitative or coercive. Walzer (1983, p. 102) has argued that the government should block 'desperate exchanges', where people contract to undertake harmful work out of desperation. Similarly, Andre (1995, p. 195) has argued that exchanges that are inherently harmful to the participants, such as the sale of body parts and narcotics, should be prohibited. More fundamentally it is claimed that the inequalities of income and wealth that exist in a market economy produce asymmetries of bargaining power between employees and employers which make many supposedly voluntary labour contracts inherently exploitative or coercive. In the words of Howarth (1994, p. 21): 'If you are the private owner of a factory in which I must work if I am to have any hope of a decent life, then you have power over me; to employ me or not, to determine my working conditions, my rate of pay, and so on.' Such arguments are used to justify minimum wage legislation to prevent workers being paid 'exploitative' wages and the prohibition of inherently exploitative employment, such as prostitution or commercial surrogacy.

It is also argued that the market is an institutional setting that leads people to make choices incongruent with their own well-being. Barber (1984), Frank (1999) and Sagoff (1988) are among those who have argued that in the marketplace people make self-centred, myopic and hedonistic choices as 'consumers' in contrast to the altruistic, thoughtful and reflective choices they make as 'citizens' in the context of democratic decision-making. Consequently, it is claimed that if democratic institutions do not impose limits on the scope of markets the result will be the creation of a 'dumbed-down', 'lowest common denominator' culture where the commercial pressures inherent to market relationships will distort and undermine the values and standards necessary to such enterprises as teaching, the arts and preservation of the environment. Government support of public service broadcasting, state subsidies to the arts, and the use of land-use planning regulation to conserve the environment are thereby justified as counter measures.

The limits to the reach of the market advocated on ethical grounds are deemed necessary not only to protect the social, cultural and moral fabric of society from the market, but also to save the market from itself; it is argued that the market has 'self-devouring' qualities that mean that an unrestrained market economy will undermine its own foundations. An unbounded market, it is argued, is unlikely to command popular support, leading to calls for its replacement with a 'more humane' economic system:

> [T]rying to work out the appropriate moral limits to markets is...centrally important because the market is only likely to appear to be legitimate and command loyalty if it is seen to have a definite sphere of legitimacy and that it is constrained from spilling over into areas of human life within which we do not wish to see goods treated as commodities. (Plant 1992, p. 120)

Furthermore, it is claimed that the trust between people and the respect for private property and the rule of law that are essential to the functioning of the market are all liable to be undermined by a market society where the great majority of relationships between people are based upon nothing more than mutual self-interest. According to Plant (1999, p. 10), in such a situation, 'the moral assumptions on which the market exchange rests could, in fact, be eroded by a culture of self-interest'. It is claimed that what is at stake in setting the appropriate limits to the market is not only the future of those areas of social life that are believed to properly exist outside the market, but also the very future of the market itself.

The *doux-commerce* thesis and beyond

It is widely held, then, that while a market economy may be more efficient than any alternative economic system it is nevertheless morally deficient; it is believed that if market forces are allowed to operate without regulation by the state then dire negative side-effects will result. It is perhaps curious that such a view of the negative moral externalities produced by the market has become so widespread because, as Hirschman (1982, p. 1464) has described, during the Enlightenment it was 'the conventional wisdom...that commerce was a civilizing agent of considerable power and range'. It is well known that the key thinkers of the Scottish Enlightenment, notably Adam Smith and David Hume, appreciated the socially and morally beneficent consequences that followed when people traded with one another in commercial markets, but it is less widely appreciated today that almost all the significant Enlightenment thinkers subscribed to what has been called the *doux-commerce* (or gentle commerce) thesis – probably the one significant exception being Rousseau. Montesquieu (1961, p. 8), for example, in his eighteenth-century classic *Spirit of the Laws*, wrote that 'it is almost a general rule that wherever manners are gentle there is commerce; and wherever there is commerce, manners are gentle'. Similarly, in *Rights of Man*, Thomas Paine (1984, p. 212) – often claimed as a forebear of socialism – described himself as 'an advocate for commerce, because I am a friend to its effects. It is a pacific system, operating to cordialize mankind'.

The *doux-commerce* thesis fell into disrepute with the advent of industrialization and urbanization at the end of the eighteenth century and, arguably more importantly, the concurrent rise of socialist and Marxist philosophy. The negative view of the social and moral impact of the market expounded by socialist thinkers still indelibly colours perceptions of the ethical impact of the market to this day, even though the foundations of this view have been eroded. The problems of industrialization and urbanization were exaggerated by contemporary and later critics of the market (see, for example, Ashton 1997), are common to all advanced economies – market or non-market – and have been largely ameliorated by the increasing wealth of industrial economies, while all the central tenets of socialism and Marxism have been discredited – to give just three examples, capitalist societies do not polarize into two increasingly separate proletariat and bourgeois classes, the labour theory of value is demonstrably false, and the history of no human society corresponds with the Marxist theory of history.

Throughout the twentieth century a small number of classical liberal and libertarian scholars revived and developed the *doux-commerce* thesis as they worked to expose the fallacies and weaknesses of the ethical critiques of the market that have achieved such widespread currency. This book brings together and synthesizes these counter-arguments and applies them to the most recent variants of these critiques of the market and to contemporary debates concerning the appropriate roles of governments and markets. By so doing, this book aims to show that a robust and compelling defence of the market can be made on ethical grounds. It will set out a positive moral case for the market that draws upon an appreciation of the epistemological role of the price mechanism in enabling people to meet the needs of others of whom they have no direct personal knowledge, and the compatibility of the market with the principle of individual self-ownership fundamental to a free society. It will be argued that a market economy is a moral economy and that the creation of a just society with a strong social and moral fabric requires the expansion of market forces as broadly and as deeply as possible. Those who believe that our future prosperity and harmony depend upon a new settlement between state and market in which government more closely regulates and sets limits to the operation of markets misunderstand the basis of both economic prosperity and social harmony: it is the continued development and extension of free, self-regulating markets that will ensure a prosperous society with strong moral foundations.

Of course, there are natural limits to the market where property rights do not and cannot exist. Walzer (1983, pp. 100–2) and Andre (1995) have identified a number of 'blocked exchanges' that principally relate to these natural limits to the market. It is clear, for example, that property rights cannot exist in love and friendship, that criminal justice cannot be bought and sold, and that the holding of political office must also be set outside the marketplace. Equally, there are social institutions, notably the family and the state, that exist independently from the marketplace. But it is not the case that an unrestrained market economy undermines these separate institutions. On the contrary, this book will argue that the market is an important 'school for virtue' and that popular participation in a market economy strengthens rather weakens these extra-market institutions.

The market and the good

Many scholars have made important contributions to our understanding of the morality of a market economy – see, for example, the classic texts by Hayek (1944, 1960, 1982a,b,c) and Nozick (1974) and the recent collection of classic papers edited by Heath (2002). But this book makes a unique contribution by setting out a positive moral case for the market that takes into account the principal ethical critiques that concern questions of social justice and the moral, cultural and social externalities of the operation of market forces. By so doing, it provides a new synthesis of many long-standing arguments and applies them to many of the latest developments in political theory and political economy.

It is also the case, as Sternberg (1999, 2000, 2003) has repeatedly noted, that many of those who have contributed to this area have not utilized ethical arguments in their apparently ethical discussions. Scholars have tended to consider whether profits are earned rather than whether they are just, whether prices are efficient communicators of information rather than whether they reflect need or desert, and whether the market maximizes pleasure and minimizes pain rather than whether such a felicific calculus is an appropriate measure of the moral impact of an economic system.

Past scholars may have appeared to neglect ethical arguments because by its very nature the market is incompatible with many of the end-state or teleological ethical perspectives utilized by moral philosophers. The market implies the deontological foundational principles of individual self-ownership and respect for private property and the rule of law, but beyond these basic principles it does not specify what ends are moral or desirable. Hence, while the market is incompatible with certain teleological end-states, such as egalitarianism, beyond these limits each individual is free to define and to pursue their own ends so long as their actions do not violate the rights of others to do likewise.

For this reason the market will inevitably appear wanting when assessed according to the criteria of a teleological ethical theory, like egalitarianism; if one believes that only an egalitarian society is a moral society then clearly the market order will appear morally deficient when compared to this ideal.

An economic system or social order that does not specify what ends are desirable need not be amoral or immoral, however. On the contrary, it is a central contention of this book that *only* an economic system or social order that does not impose teleological criteria on its citizens can be considered moral; any attempt to impose a particular set of ends upon people must violate their basic right to self-ownership and self-determination.

The ethical case for the market made in this book does not rest upon the acceptance or advocacy of any particular set of values or moral schema. Rather, it is claimed that while the market is incompatible with certain end-states, for example where private property rights do not exist or cannot be realized, it is also compatible with a wide range of different conceptions of the good. The market is as applicable to a society of selfless altruists as it is to a society of selfish hedonists. The ethical case for the market rests upon the claim that if we do wish to help other people of whom we have no direct personal knowledge, then the market is the most efficacious mechanism for so doing, that the market gives the greatest possible scope for individuals to determine their own destiny, that only the distribution of income and wealth arising from the impersonal workings of the market can be considered just and that the market is a self-regulating and self-replenishing institution.

The structure of the book

The main body of this book begins by setting out the positive ethical benefits that come from participation in a market economy. Chapter 2, *Markets and Ethics*, will show that only the market provision of goods and services is compatible with the principle of individual self-ownership that must form the basis of a free society. It is because in the marketplace people pursue their own self-conceived ends that the market is able to utilize the knowledge of people's needs and preferences that is captured and communicated by the price mechanism to achieve unprecedented efficiency gains. Furthermore, it is only when people respond to price signals that they are able to meet the needs of people of whom they have no direct personal knowledge. Hence, it will be argued that if altruism is applicable at all at a societal level it can only be realized by responding to the price signals generated by the market.

This positive account of the ethics of the market will then be further developed and elucidated by engagement with the most important ethical critiques of the market. The first of these critiques concerns the epistemological function of the price mechanism central to the ethical account set out in Chapter 2. In Chapter 3, *Prices and Needs*, three challenges to the claims made in the previous chapter will be addressed: that many of the prices that exist in real world market economies do not reflect people's needs but rather reflect the purchasing power of different individuals; that there are some values that cannot be translated into monetary prices, and that the price mechanism does not perform the coordinating function that was claimed of it in Chapter 2. This chapter will then show why each of these objections should be rejected.

Having established the crucial place of the epistemological function of market prices in an ethical account of the market, the next two chapters will address questions of 'social justice'. Arguments relating to the differential purchasing power of different individuals resulting from the inequalities of income and wealth that were raised in Chapter 3 will be addressed in Chapter 4, *Distribution and Justice*. This chapter will show why only the distribution of income and wealth determined by the market can be considered just. It will also argue that material inequalities are an essential part of the process of wealth creation and for this reason they can be said to benefit the least advantaged and least well-off. It will also be shown that the economic inequalities that exist within the market are dynamic rather than static; it is not the case that the rich get richer while the poor get poorer. This chapter will argue, however, that the state should guarantee every citizen a minimum basic income as a safety net to ensure that no individual faces destitution for any reason.

Chapter 5, *Exploitation and Coercion*, will address a second dimension of 'social justice': the claim that many of the voluntary exchanges that take place in the marketplace are in reality founded upon exploitation and coercion. This chapter will show that many of the activities fundamental to the market that are intuitively believed by many to be exploitative, such as using other people as a means of achieving one's own ends and arbitrage, are in fact an essential feature of any advanced economy. It will also be shown that bargaining in a market economy does not take place between monopsonistic employers and individual employees, thus leading to exploitation and coercion, but rather a market economy is characterized by a multiplicity of firms who compete to employ the most productive workers. The chapter will set out the limits to individual choice that exist in any social situation where people's legitimate choices impact on others. It will be shown that a choice is not coerced even if people believe they have no plausible alternative if that situation has arisen as a result of the legitimate choices of others.

After engaging with critiques of the market relating to 'social justice' the final two chapters in the main body of the book will address the social and cultural impact of the market. Chapter 6, *Culture and*

Well-being, will engage with the claim that the market is an institutional setting in which people make shallow, selfish and myopic choices as 'consumers' that leave them trapped on a 'hedonic treadmill' on which they pursue material goals in the vain hope that they will bring fulfilment. It will show that this is a completely erroneous depiction of the market process. The market is not an institutional setting in which atomistic individuals make decisions without regard to the needs and preferences of others, but is an institutional setting in which people must take into account other people's needs and preferences if they are to achieve their own ends. Critics of materialism and economic growth more generally neglect the enormous benefits that come from material prosperity, such as better healthcare, better education and increased leisure time. Finally, it will be shown that the market does not produce a 'lowest common denominator' culture in which the most base and shallow cultural products predominate, but instead leads to the production of a wide array of (what might be termed) high and low cultural products.

Chapter 7, *Morality and Commerce*, will rebut the argument that the market undermines the very social institutions upon which its own future functioning depends. This chapter will show that the market is an institution that positively contributes to the generation of trust between people and respect for private property and the rule of law. Success in the market is dependent upon the ability to meet the needs of others combined with a reputation for probity and trustworthiness; few people would be willing to enter into exchanges with an individual who did not possess such a positive reputation. Even in the more impersonal, non-iterated exchanges that characterize an advanced market economy, economic institutions have developed to supply the 'moral capital' necessary for successful market exchanges. Finally, this chapter will set out the wider role of the market as part of the framework through which the moral fabric of society is constantly shared, renewed and replenished.

A short concluding chapter will briefly summarize the principal conclusions of the book and suggest why the positive ethical account of the market made in this work is not more widely accepted.

2
Markets and Ethics

This chapter will show that a compelling ethical case can be made for the market that takes into account questions of self-ownership, economic efficiency and the altruistic desire to help other people. While the classical Marxist and socialist critics of capitalism believed that capitalism was both inefficient and immoral in comparison to the socialist alternative, today it is more frequently alleged that although capitalism may be more efficient than any alternative economic system, it is nevertheless a form of economic organization that encourages and rewards selfishness, dishonesty and other forms of immoral behaviour (for example, Plant 1999; Wilson 1995).

Perhaps it is not surprising that such a negative perception of the morality of the market has become commonplace given that many of the classical economists who first set out the philosophical foundations of the market appeared to accept that egoism and selfishness were integral parts of the market process. Adam Smith, for example, famously described self-love as the principal motivating force of market participants:

> It is not from the benevolence of the butcher, the brewer, or the baker that we expect our dinner, but from their regard to their own interest. We address ourselves, not to their humanity but to their self-love, and never talk to them of our own necessities but of their advantages. (Smith 1981, pp. 26–7)

Similarly, Bernard Mandeville, one of the most important precursors of Smith's account of the market, appeared to describe the market as a system whose successful operation depended upon and then rewarded the avarice and covetousness of its participants. In Mandeville's (1988, pp. 20–1) poetic description of the prosperous 'beehive' of the market, 'All Trades and Places knew some Cheat, No Calling was without Deceit' and every individual was motivated by 'Sloth, Lust, Avarice and Pride'. Classical and now neo-classical economics are both founded upon the assumption that people's principal motivation is to pursue their own self-interest and hence it is assumed that it is self-interest that properly drives a market economy. As stated in a standard late nineteenth-century economics text: 'the first principle of Economics is that every agent is actuated by self-interest' (Edgeworth 1881, p. 16). It is little wonder, perhaps, that Ruskin (1934, p. 14n) could write that anyone who could read the classical economists without repulsion must have entered into an 'entirely damned state of soul'.

This chapter will reject the view that the market is dependent upon the immorality of individual actors. It will argue that the principles by which a market economy operates are equally applicable to a society of perfect altruists or completely selfish egoists: even the most selfless individual, who has decided to dedicate their life to helping others, should utilize market mechanisms to achieve their ends. It is only when individuals seek to maximize their personal profits in response to price signals generated by the market that the actions of many disparate economic actors can be coordinated, that resources can be allocated efficiently and that individuals can learn about the needs of other people of whom they have no direct personal knowledge. Furthermore, the market is the only economic system that is compatible with the principle of individual self-ownership that must lie at the heart of a free society.

Plan of the chapter

This chapter will first show that only the market provision of goods and services is compatible with the principle of individual self-ownership. It will then set out the relationship between the fact that the market enables people to pursue their own self-conceived ends and the unprecedented level of efficiency achieved by market economies. Economic efficiency can be achieved only where individuals seek to maximize their pecuniary profits, that is, where people seek to ensure that the benefits of economic activity exceed the costs.

Moreover, it is only by pursuing profits in the marketplace that people can meet the needs of others of whom they have no direct personal knowledge. Hence, an individual who wishes to be altruistic at a societal level should pursue this end by seeking to maximize their pecuniary profits. While the generation of profit is undoubtedly a public good, this chapter will finally consider whether a moral distinction should be drawn between those people who use the profits they have made to fund charitable endeavours and those who engage in gratuitous consumption.

The market, self-ownership and 'exit'

The fundamental principle of a free society is individual self-ownership: each individual person and their property are sacrosanct and cannot be violated by anyone else except where that person has first violated the property rights of another. This position was classically set out as far back as the seventeenth century in Locke's (1993, p. 287) second treatise of government: 'every Man has a Property in his own Person. This no Body has any Right to but himself. The Labour of his Body, and the Work of his Hands, we may say, are properly his.' In his classic essay *On Liberty* John Stuart Mill (1985, p. 69) also gave an account of the principle of self-ownership:

> The only part of the conduct of anyone for which [the individual] is amenable to society is that which concerns others. In the part which merely concerns himself, his independence is, of right, absolute. Over himself, over his own body and mind, the individual is sovereign.

The principle of self-ownership implies that 'each individual possesses original moral rights over her own body, faculties, talents, and energies' and hence it involves a 'perception of the moral inviolability of persons ... whose lives and well-being are of separate and irreplaceable moral importance' (Mack 2002, p. 76).

Accordingly, it is judged that individuals should be free to determine and pursue their own ends, that, in the words of Hayek (1948a, p. 15), 'people are and ought to be guided in their actions by *their* interest and desires ... they ought to be allowed to strive for whatever *they* think desirable'. A free society requires that individuals are able to pursue their own self-conceived ends, rather than have ends imposed upon them by others, whether politicians, bureaucrats, majorities or gangsters. It is believed, as Isaiah Berlin (1969, p. 137) described in a particularly memorable phrase, that to use people for ends other than those that they have themselves conceived 'is, in effect, to treat them as sub-human, to behave as if their ends are less ultimate and sacred than my own'.

It has been suggested that a distinction should be made between the right of self-ownership of one's own person and the right of self-ownership of one's property. It is argued that rights to the ownership of property, or to certain types of property, or to the income derived from certain types of property, do not have the same moral status as ownership of one's self (for example, Christman 1991; Cohen 1995; Otsuka 2003). It is contended that while an individual may be entirely sovereign over their body, the external resources of the world are another matter entirely, so that, 'Perhaps even if we possess a libertarian right of ownership over ourselves, we can only ever come to have a less full right of ownership over land and other worldly resources' (Otsuka 2003, p. 21). On this basis, it is claimed that redistributive taxation and even egalitarianism may be reconciled with the principle of self-ownership.

There is a qualitative difference in the moral claim that an individual has to ownership of their person and to ownership of their property; murder and rape are more heinous crimes than theft. But that distinction should not mask the fact that theft is a crime and that the ability to dispose of one's property as one chooses is an integral part of the moral status attributed to human beings in a free society.

The right to self-ownership extends to a person's property because of the connection between the acquisition of property and one's person. In the classical Lockean sense, as will be discussed in more detail in Chapter 4, a property right is established when a person applies their labour to a natural resource in the state of nature. It is because each individual has a property right in their own person that when the labour of their body is mixed with the natural products of the earth that which is produced is legitimately their property (Locke 1993, Chapter 5). In contemporary terms, we acquire property rights via our labour indirectly by earning money. Whether we earn money by working in an office or by investing our capital wisely, there is an intrinsic connection between ownership of one's person and ownership of one's property. It is on this basis that Nozick (1974, p. 172) argued that compulsory taxation involved 'a shift from the classical liberals' notion of self-ownership to a notion of (partial) property rights in *other* people', because to forcibly take another person's property was to force that person to work for purposes other than their own and hence in some sense to take possession of that person's body.

Furthermore, self-ownership extends to property because individuals can only freely pursue their own self-conceived ends if they are at liberty to use their property as they see fit. Where individuals may only spend their money on certain goods and services, or must surrender a portion of their income to be spent on ends determined by others, then they cannot be said to exercise their right to pursue ends that they themselves have chosen. It is only where individuals are able to freely make use of their property that they can pursue their own ends as truly autonomous moral agents.

While the notion of self-ownership will intuitively appear to many to provide an accurate account of the moral status of individual men and women – the concept clearly forms the basis of the belief that murder, slavery and theft, among other crimes, are morally wrong – it has nevertheless been subject to concerted scholarly attack because of the serious challenge the concept poses to redistributive and egalitarian theories (a challenge that forms the basis of Chapter 4).

In addition to the attempts to drive a philosophical wedge between ownership of one's self and ownership of one's property, it has been argued that the claim that each individual has a right to self-ownership falsely inflates a concept that is the relativist product of the particular social context of contemporary liberal democracies into a universal standard: the principle of self-ownership is a product of the social context of liberal democratic societies, but advocates of the principle want to mould societies around it, confusing the background structure of society with the beliefs that it produces and ignoring the fact that limits to self-ownership, for example in the form of compulsory taxation, are also established and prior parts of the social context from which it has emerged (Wolff 1991, p. 141; this criticism is in large part derived from Rawls 1977, 1999).

It is certainly true that the concept of self-ownership is a product of contemporary liberal democratic societies where the belief in the sanctity of the individual has developed a hitherto unprecedented hegemony, but the fact that a belief is socially contingent does not invalidate it as a means of making sense of or organizing the world; were this the case then practically the entire edifice of civilization would be invalidated.

The concept of self-ownership has developed simultaneously with the liberal democratic state and a state clearly is a pre-requisite to the rule of law essential to the realization of self-ownership. This means that the principle of self-ownership can only ever be applied imperfectly; a compromise must be made between people's right to ownership of their property and the necessity of funding even a minimal state out of general taxation. Hence, the concept of self-ownership should be understood in the context of the broader background structure from which it has emerged.

The realization of the greatest possible sphere of individual freedom does require that all individuals surrender a share of their property to the state, but the principle of self-ownership requires that such resources should be requisitioned via a universal flat rate income or sales tax that does discriminate against particular individuals or categories of people. In the real world freedom can never be absolute, but a society is more free where the state takes ten per cent of everyone's income than where it takes sixty per cent of one person's earnings and forty per cent of anothers'.

As will be discussed in more detail in Chapter 4, the concept of self-ownership cannot be reconciled with redistributive taxation, which should be understood as a later and counter historical development, arguably akin to theft because it involves taking one person's property for the benefit of another.

Only the market provision of goods and services is compatible with the principle of self-ownership. When goods are supplied in private markets, every individual has the option to 'exit' from a particular transaction if it is not congruent with their ends. If an individual does not approve of a firm's employment practices they can choose to frequent their competitors; vegetarians can choose not to buy meat, and those who do not like the taste of a particular soft drink can purchase an alternative. The power of exit is one of the most important disciplines of the marketplace: not only are consumers not required to purchase goods and services that do not correspond with their own ends, firms that fail to meet consumers' demands will be forced into bankruptcy (Hirschman 1970).

By contrast, when goods and services are supplied by non-market means, that is, as public goods provided by the government and paid for out of general taxation, no such exit option exists. Unless collective decisions are taken unanimously, the majority has the power to force its ends upon the minority and the minority have no exit option. In such a situation, pacifists must pay for nuclear weapons, cyclists must contribute to the construction of new motorways and vegans are required to fund live animal experiments in government laboratories. When goods and services are provided by non-market means, people are required to work towards ends that they do not share. In other words, the provision of goods and services via compulsory taxation amounts to the forced appropriation of people's property and hence of people's labour for ends other than their own.

The provision of goods and services by non-market means not only requires people to pay for goods and services that they do not want, it also means that people must accept the level of supply chosen by the majority. If a local authority constructs an olympic-size swimming pool, for example, residents with no desire to use it will be required to pay for it, while those who would rather pay for a more modest pool will have to pay for the olympic facility.

To say that in the market individuals have greater freedom and autonomy to pursue their own ends than in any other economic system does not mean that in a market economy any individual has the absolute freedom to do *whatever* they want irrespective of the ends and wants of others, nor does it mean that individuals formulate ends in isolation from other people. On the contrary, individuals may not infringe the rights of others in pursuit of their ends, and any person's ends are ultimately only realizable to the extent that they can be reconciled with the ends of others. Hence, a man who wishes to be a fabulously wealthy pop star can only achieve this goal if he can persuade other people to purchase his music, and a woman who aspires to life as a supermodel can only realize her ambition if she can find employment on the most prestigious catwalks of the world.

The market is a social process in which individuals learn that their ends can be achieved only if they can be reconciled with those of other people. Hence, in the market individuals re-evaluate and reformulate their plans in the light of the knowledge of other people's ends communicated by the price mechanism: an aspiring racing driver becomes a car dealer; a would-be footballer trains as a fitness instructor and a resting actor works as a waiter. By requiring people to revise their ends in the light of the information about the ends of others communicated by price signals, the market process spontaneously dovetails a myriad of different and frequently competing ends and values into an apparently seamless web of coordinated economic activity (for example, Hayek 1944, 1948a; Kirzner 1992, 2000).

A free society, then, is one in which individuals have the freedom to pursue their own self-conceived ends in every possible sphere. Hence, as Milton Friedman (2002) described, the appropriate role of business in a free society is to pursue its shareholders' interests – whatever they may be – within the law, and to impose any other notion of 'social responsibility' upon those individuals who happen to be employees or shareholders of commercial organizations constitutes an infringement of their right to pursue their own ends.

While every economic system operates within an institutional framework provided by the state that must be funded out of general taxation, within the context of that framework only the market provision of goods and services, where people have the option to exit from transactions they do not wish to participate in, is compatible with the principle of self-ownership; by comparison, any other economic system involves a diminution of individual liberty.

Prosperity, self-ownership and the market process

As described in the introductory chapter, today it is rarely disputed that the market produces efficiency gains and hence generates a level of material prosperity that no other economic system can match. Indeed, there is clear empirical evidence of the correlation between the existence of a market economy and material prosperity. The most comprehensive international empirical study of the relation-ship between economic freedom and prosperity, undertaken annu-ally by the Heritage Foundation, has shown over a ten-year period that those countries with market economies (defined in terms of established private property rights, sound money and minimal government intervention in the economy) were the most econom-ically prosperous: 'The countries with the most economic freedom . . . have higher rates of long-term economic growth and are more prosperous than are those with less economic freedom' (Miles, Feulner and O'Grady 2004, p. 1).

Over the longer term, the record of market economies is even more impressive. During the course of the twentieth century, market economies attained levels of growth that were historically unprecedented, while planned economies suffered relative and very often absolute economic decline. The prosperity that the market generates has important social consequences: only economic growth can enable large numbers of people to be simultaneously taken out of poverty and can facilitate the development of modern systems of healthcare and education provision (Henderson 2004; Norberg 2001).

A possible counterview may be found in the empirical research that has shown a slightly positive (though not statistically significant) correlation between economic growth and a large public sector (for example, Agell, Lindh and Ohlsson 1997). This result need not contradict the claim that economic freedom produces prosperity, however, given that only countries that have reached a certain level of prosperity are able to fund a modern welfare state, and the modern welfare state has everywhere been supported by an advanced market economy. Hence, what such analysis cannot show is how much more impressive economic growth may have been without the presence of a large public sector weighing down the economy.

While the efficiency gains and resultant prosperity generated by the market are widely recognized, the relationship between the principle of self-ownership at the heart of a free society and the material prosperity created by the market is less well appreciated. It is because in a market economy individuals are free to pursue their own self-conceived ends and thereby to utilize their own personal knowledge that a market economy achieves such a high level of efficiency in its use of resources. To understand why this is the case it is necessary to first present an account of how the market produces economic prosperity that is rooted in the requirements of an advanced division of labour.

The division of labour, coordination and knowledge

An advanced division of labour is the most important pre-requisite of economic prosperity. It facilitates the introduction of economies of scale and increased specialization that allow the production of far more goods than could possibly be produced otherwise. Adam Smith (1981, pp. 14–15) famously used the example of pin-making to illustrate the importance of the division of labour to increased productivity. Whereas one skilled individual working alone could make perhaps twenty pins a day, a pin factory employing ten men who each worked on two or three specialist tasks in the manufacturing process produced some forty-eight thousand pins a day. Each one worker could therefore be said to have produced approximately four thousand eight hundred pins per day, an enormous gain on what could have been achieved if the whole process had been attempted alone. When the principle of the division of labour is applied throughout society, the efficiency gains and increased productivity foster economic prosperity.

An advanced division of labour implies the existence of trade. Individuals can only concentrate on a small number of specialist tasks if they are able to exchange the products of their labour for the products of other people's labour. International trade facilitates economies of scale and specialization on a global scale, allowing countries to focus on the production of the goods and services in which they have a comparative advantage, which can then be traded with the goods and services produced by other countries. The wealth of nations is created via this process of international commerce built on the global division of labour that enables each country to enjoy a bounty that could not be produced by any single self-sufficient country.

An advanced division of labour, particularly on a global scale, requires the coordination of the activities of many millions of people: screws moulded in a factory in Sao Paulo must fit the requirements of a shipbuilder in Yokohama; computer software developed in Seattle must meet the needs of a small business in Madrid, and spring onions grown in Egypt must arrive fresh on the supermarket shelves of London. Moreover, not only must the actions of many millions of disparate people be coordinated, if resources are to be used efficiently the value of outputs (goods and services) produced must equal or exceed the value of inputs (factors of production) used to produce them. If the costs of production exceed the value of the good produced, then impoverishment will result, while an economy that uses resources less efficiently than another will experience relative impoverishment.

The attainment of such an efficient use of resources in an advanced economy can only be achieved where individuals and firms utilize price signals in the pursuit of their own self-conceived ends. Without market prices it is impossible to arrive at an accurate relative valuation of the many millions of different goods and services, and the many million factors of production that may be used to create those goods and services. Such a monumental feat is beyond the comprehension of any single mind, group of minds working together or super-computer, because it would require knowledge of all the needs and preferences of the many millions of people who constitute an advanced economy, and the relative urgency of those needs and preferences, information that is not only stupendously complex, but is also highly subjective and frequently tacit (for example, Boettke 2001; Lavoie 1985; O'Driscoll and Rizzo 1996).

As Hayek (1948c, p. 50) wrote, in understanding the operation of a modern, complex economy, 'the problem of the *division of knowledge*' is 'quite analogous to, and at least as important as, the problem of the division of labour'. The knowledge essential to economic coordination does not exist as a cohesive block that any individual, group of individuals or even super-computer, could comprehend or process, because such knowledge 'never exists in concentrated or integrated form but solely as the dispersed bits of incomplete and frequently contradictory knowledge which all the separate individuals possess' (Hayek 1948b, p. 77).

In a market economy, however, the price mechanism effortlessly and constantly processes and communicates this information. The prices of goods and services on the high streets and supermarket shelves reflect the marginal utility and opportunity cost of the production or delivery of each good or service. Individual plans and actions are spontaneously coordinated when they respond to the price signals generated by the market: a multitude of goods and services are bought and sold every second by producers and consumers who may have no personal knowledge of one another but are able to dovetail their actions together by responding to market prices.

Coordination within a market economy does not imply that all individuals work towards the same goal – on the contrary, many firms will be active competitors – but that the actions of a myriad of different individuals frequently working in ignorance of one another generate a dynamic, complex economic system in a way that none of them intend or can foresee. Hayek (1948b, p. 87) hailed the ability of the price mechanism to perform this coordinating function as a 'marvel':

> I am convinced that if it were the result of deliberate human design, and if the people guided by the price changes understood that their decisions have significance far beyond their immediate aim, this mechanism would have been acclaimed as one of the greatest triumphs of the human mind.

The price mechanism is only able to utilize dispersed, tacit and subjective knowledge *because* it is not the result of conscious deliberation. Any attempt to 'improve' upon the price mechanism by deliberate or rational planning will fail because it must utilize less knowledge; it is limited by what can be comprehended by the single mind or group of minds that have designed the 'improvement'.

The price system utilizes the personal knowledge that individuals reveal when they pursue their own self-conceived ends in the marketplace. If people did not pursue their own self-conceived ends then the knowledge of individual needs and preferences, and their relative urgency, essential to economic efficiency would not be expressed or revealed and could not be utilized. Hence, an economy not founded upon the principle of self-ownership could not achieve the same level of efficiency.

To say that the market is the most effective means of determining the value of different goods and services (and the factors of production that compose those different goods and services) does not imply that all market prices are perfect, that market participants never make errors, nor that markets always (or ever) attain equilibrium. On the contrary, markets work more effectively than any other means of economic organization precisely *because* they enable market participants to heuristically learn from their mistakes and the mistakes of others. When a production manager within a planned economy sets an incorrect price or makes an inefficient allocation of the resources at their disposal, for example, they have no way of knowing that an error has been made, let alone how to correct it. The existence of profits and losses within a market economy, however, provides information as to the success or failure of different courses of action that facilitates heuristic learning among market participants. It is because – contra the neo-classical model – markets exist in a constant state of disequilibrium that within a market context opportunities exist for individuals to modify their actions, rather than being condemned to repeat the same choices over and over again (Hayek 1948b; Kirzner 1992, 2000).

The power of market prices in attaining economic coordination is such that all serious attempts to replace the market system have involved the introduction of a system of quasi-prices, or market socialism (for example, Lange and Taylor 1938). Unfortunately, the market socialist solution fails because the accounting prices set by the planners and bureaucrats charged with managing the economy cannot perform the epistemological function demanded of them in the absence of fully functioning markets in consumer and capital goods; prices can only reflect the relative value of different goods and services (and the factors of production required to produce those goods and services) if they are generated by genuine markets driven by the polycentric choices of consumers and producers (for example, Boettke 2001; Hayek 1982d; Reynolds 1998; Rothbard 1991; Steele 1992).

By allowing individuals the freedom to pursue their own self-conceived ends, the market process translates the subjective, personal knowledge possessed by each person into market prices that facilitate the coordination of the actions of many individuals who have no direct knowledge of one another. There is, then, no dichotomy or choice to be made between freedom and efficiency in the ethical case for the market: if individual liberty were not at the heart of the market process, this personal knowledge could not be utilized and the resultant economic efficiency could not be attained.

Profits, altruism and the market

The positive ethical case for the market set out in this chapter began by noting that only the market provision of goods and services is compatible with the principle of individual self-ownership. It then went on to describe how it is because in a market economy individuals pursue their own self-conceived ends under the guidance of the price mechanism and therefore utilize their own personal, subjective knowledge that the market is able to achieve efficiency gains that no other economic system can match. The final part of the positive ethical case for the market set out in this chapter concerns the fact that the principles upon which the market operates apply equally irrespective of whether an individual's ends are selfish or altruistic. Indeed, if we wish to be altruistic at a societal level – to help other people of whom we have no direct personal knowledge – the most efficacious way to do so is by pursuing the price signals generated by the market; that is, by maximizing our pecuniary profits.

The ability of the market to coordinate the actions of many dispersed individuals via the price mechanism is equally relevant to a society composed wholly of saintly altruists or one composed entirely of selfish egoists because both altruistic and selfish ends can only be realized if resources are used efficiently and this can only happen if firms and individuals engage in profit-maximizing behaviour.

The generation of profits simply means that the value of goods produced exceeds the costs required to produce them. The more profits that are generated, the greater the efficiency gains that have been achieved, the more goods that can be produced, and therefore the more needs that can be satisfied, from a given set of resources. Hence, as Mises (1981, p. 124) stated: 'Between production for profit and production for needs there is no contrast.'

While Adam Smith (1981, p. 26–7) famously described 'self-love' as the motivating force driving economic coordination in commercial society, in reality the key is not that individuals are selfishly motivated, but that individuals are motivated to respond to the price signals generated by the market. Economic coordination demands that people are entrepreneurially alert, which can only be the case if individuals pursue ends that they themselves believe to be important, irrespective of whether those ends are altruistic or selfish. As Kirzner (1992, pp. 204–8) described:

> Persons with no interests or goals will not tend to discover changes in external conditions that favour or threaten the realization of interests or goals. Alertness without some degree of purposefulness is simply and totally implausible. Self-interest...switches on one's awareness of hitherto unnoticed disappointing conditions, or hitherto unnoticed opportunities for gain...The point to be stressed is that it is one's *own* purposefulness which inspires one's actions and excites one's alertness. One's purpose may be altruistic or otherwise; one's interest in achieving one's (possibly altruistic) goals switches on one's alertness to opportunities for advancing those goals.

Smith's description of the importance of self-love to the operation of the market should be properly understood as highlighting the polycentric, decentralized basis of economic coordination and hence the importance of individual motivation to observe and respond to the needs and demands of others – as communicated by the price mechanism. If individuals are to respond to the price signals generated by the market then they must be alert to the world around them and how they can integrate their own ends (whether altruistic or selfish) with the ends of others.

Profit as a public good

In the marketplace an individual need not be altruistically motivated in order that their actions benefit others. An unintended consequence of the self-interested pursuit of profit by individuals within a market economy is the satisfaction of more needs than would be possible if people had consciously striven to achieve a similarly socially beneficial outcome. The actions of self-interested, profit-maximizing individuals have given the populations of the developed world access to an array of goods and services that their ancestors could not have even dreamed of, such as fresh meat with every meal, washing machines, cars, personal computers and so on – the list is almost endless. The profits to be made from the supply of such goods are indicative of the fact that large numbers of people value their production more than they value alternative uses of their resources. By contrast, socialist economies that have attempted to consciously meet people's needs through central planning mechanisms – what might be regarded as the institutionalization of altruism – have created impoverishment and economic collapse. People who attempt to meet the needs of others through deliberate means, for example through acts of charity, can only help those relatively few people of whom they have direct personal knowledge. Therefore, as Hayek (1982b, p. 145) described, an individual who responds to the price signals generated by the market:

> [I]s led to benefit more people by aiming at the largest gain that he could than if he concentrated on the satisfaction of the needs of known persons. He is led by the invisible hand of the market to bring the succour of modern conveniences to the poorest homes he does not even know.

Those individuals who have established profit-maximizing firms in order to self-interestedly reap the pecuniary rewards that follow from supplying goods and services will have satisfied the needs of more people via the market than their contemporaries who have deliberately attempted to help people by engaging in charitable endeavours.

This is not to suggest that price signals heuristically generated in the marketplace perfectly represent the needs of different individuals or that profits perfectly represent the social contribution made by business enterprises. Profits and prices may be 'contaminated' or distorted by externalities and government regulation so that they do not accurately represent the costs and benefits of the actions of a firm or individual (Henderson 2004, pp. 108–10). The solution to these problems is to develop and extend property rights so that contractual relationships may capture all the costs and benefits involved (Meadowcroft 2004) and the minimization of government regulation to ensure that profits reflect the genuine costs and benefits of commercial enterprises.

Prices can never be 'perfect' – rather they are a guide to the subjective preferences of producers and consumers at a particular moment in time – but they are nevertheless the most effective means of surmounting the epistemological barriers that confront any attempt to broaden the scope of our actions to individuals of whom we have no direct personal knowledge.

While it is possible and virtuous to altruistically help known individuals – for example when care is given to family members, friends or even a person in the street in need of help – if altruism is applicable at all at a societal level it is only possible by responding to the information of other people's needs and preferences communicated by the price mechanism. When a person responds to the needs of people of whom they have direct personal knowledge they can only respond to a tiny fraction of society's needs and have no way of effectively evaluating the relative urgency of those needs. But when an individual responds to the price signals generated by the market they are able to respond to the needs of the countless different individuals dispersed throughout the economy that they could not possibly consciously comprehend. Thus, whether an individual 'is completely selfish or the most perfect altruist', without the guidance of price signals generated by the market, 'the human needs for which he *can* effectively care are an almost negligible fraction of the needs of all members of society' (Hayek 1948a, p. 14).

The profit motive may be perceived as a public good that has important and far-reaching socially beneficent consequences. In a market economy, a person faced with a choice between two alternative courses of action, one of which will bring a large monetary reward, while the other will bring only a small return, should *altruistically* choose the course of action that returns the largest possible monetary profit. Maximizing profits ensures that resources are used to maximum efficiency and also enables individuals and firms to meet the needs of the greatest number people of whom they have no direct personal knowledge.

Consumption and charity in the disposal of profits

It has been argued, however, that while an altruistic and a self-interested individual should both seek to maximize their pecuniary profits in the marketplace, the crucial difference between a person motivated by altruism and one motivated by self-interest 'is surely what the former does with his gains' (Brittan 1995, p. 61). An altruist, it is argued, should utilize the price mechanism to maximize the pecuniary rewards of his activities, but should then 'transfer his profits to those whom he believes most in need or in other ways deserving' (Brittan 1995, pp. 61–2; see also Kirzner 2004).

While one may quibble as to whether a person's motives can ever be truly altruistic or whether charitable giving always has more to do with the 'warm-glow' that an individual derives from helping others (for example, Andreoni 1990; Batson 1987), it is hard to disagree with the contention that an individual who uses their profits to endow an art gallery or to fund campaigns against malaria in Africa, for example, should be considered more virtuous than a person who spends their profits on luxury holidays or gargantuan meals at the most expensive restaurants.

Without doubt, there are emergencies or crisis situations that fall outside the scope of market relationships when it will be possible to objectively ascertain the needs of people who are not personally known to us without reference to price signals, or, indeed, where the market may have ceased to operate and price signals cannot therefore be utilized. In the immediate aftermath of a natural disaster such as an earthquake, for example, it is quite clear that people require the most basic needs of food, clothing and shelter. It is undeniable that the provision of aid and assistance in the event of such disasters is necessary and virtuous and that in such a situation (what might be termed) 'societal altruism' will be appropriate and applicable.

But it should not be forgotten that production and consumption in the marketplace form part of a virtuous circle through which people learn about the needs and preferences of others and resources are allocated to where they are most needed to respond to those needs and preferences. If people did not 'selfishly' consume the goods and services that they desire, then other individuals would have no opportunity to learn about their needs and preferences in order to (self-interestedly or altruistically) satisfy them. Given that altruism requires that other people have self-interested concerns that can be placed ahead of one's own, it is clear that altruism (if it is possible at all at a societal level) requires some mechanism to communicate information about other people's needs and desires. In a complex, advanced economy this function is performed most efficiently by the price mechanism. Hence, it is only when people engage in production *and* consumption that the price signals gener-ated by the market accurately reflect the interests of all the many dispersed members of society. Indeed, given that the very purpose of production is to enable consumption to take place, it is not clear why consumption should be considered morally questionable *per se*.

It is also the case, as discussed above, that while an individual in an advanced economy may altruistically use their profits to help certain known individuals or causes, it is practically impossible to deliberately respond to the needs of those individuals of whom they have no direct personal knowledge (who will make up the majority of their peers) other than by responding to market price signals. Direct altruism that involves helping known individuals or causes must therefore be undertaken in the knowledge that there are likely to be unknown others whose need is greater; charitable benevolence is limited by the donor's partial knowledge of other people and their needs. By contrast, the market transcends the boundaries of such personal knowledge and, possibly, prejudice. As Coase (1976, p. 544) described:

> The great advantage of the market is that it is able to use the strength of self-interest to offset the weakness and partiality of benevolence, so that those who are unknown, unattractive, or unimportant, will have their wants served.

It may be considered morally preferable 'to invest one's fortune in instruments making it possible to produce more at smaller costs than to distribute it among the poor, or to cater for the needs of thousands of unknown people rather than to provide for the needs of a few known neighbours' (Hayek 1982b, pp. 144–5). While charity is important and benevolent, it should be undertaken in the knowledge that it is a limited and partial means of helping others. Charitable activity should therefore be principally directed towards intervention in crisis situations and efforts to extend the scope of the market to those excluded from its reach so that they too can benefit from the freedom and prosperity that it brings.

Finally, if the belief that giving money to known individuals and good causes is morally superior to responding to the impersonal signals of the market were to become endemic throughout a given society, this may lead people to take action that was socially pernicious. The population of a prosperous, capitalist society could be persuaded by individuals of high moral standing to reject the abstract principles of the market and replace them with an economic order that sought to deliberately respond to the visible needs of its members. Any attempt to organize society accordingly would, however, lead to economic collapse and the destitution of the great majority of the population. Hayek (1960, p. 67) foresaw the possibility that in this way a society 'may destroy itself by following the teaching of what it regards as its best men, perhaps saintly figures unquestionably guided by the most unselfish ideals'.

While at first sight it would appear accurate that the distinction between an altruistic and a selfish person should concern what each does with their profits, rather than the fact that each aims to maximize profits in the first place, closer examination reveals that caution should be exercised before making such a judgement. While it should not be said that 'greed is good', it is the case that profit is good, while the benefits of charity may be relatively limited. Moreover, it should not be forgotten that it is the prosperity that the market creates that makes charity possible on the scale that facilitates intervention at times of crisis.

Conclusion

This chapter has presented a positive account of the ethics of the market. There have been three basic dimensions to this account. First, only the market provision of goods and services is compatible with a free society in which each individual has a right of self-ownership. Second, because in the marketplace each individual pursues their own self-conceived ends under the guidance of price signals the market is able to utilize the personal knowledge possessed by each individual to achieve an unparalleled level of efficiency and hence is able to meet more needs from a given set of resources than any alternative economic system. Third, it is only when individuals respond to the abstract signals provided by the price mechanism that they are able to meet the needs of the many disparate individuals who constitute a complex, advanced society. For these reasons, whether an individual is completely altruistic or wholly selfish, the principles upon which the market operates are equally relevant to the pursuit of their ends. Moreover, if an individual wishes to be altruistic at a societal level by meeting the needs of those people of whom they have no direct personal knowledge, the most effective way to do this is by maximizing their pecuniary profits in the marketplace.

This final argument is likely to appear counter-intuitive – perhaps even offensive – to many. But it is nevertheless the case that a person who wishes to selflessly put themselves at the service of others should do so by observing and responding to the price signals generated by the market; that an individual who wishes to selfishly maximize their pecuniary rewards should follow exactly the same course of action does not invalidate this fact. Rather, it is indicative of the power of the market as a force for good that it leads people to work for the benefit of others irrespective of their motives.

It may seem that if this argument were put into practice it would lead to the creation of a callous society of selfish individuals whose only concern was the generation of personal pecuniary profits. This objection will be considered in detail in Chapter 7, but it should be emphasized here that this chapter has not argued against altruism, but rather has challenged widely held assumptions about how altruistic ends can be attained at a societal level. Direct altruistic acts of helping – whether giving encouragement, financial support or some other material assistance – are appropriate and virtuous at a personal level between individuals who are known to one another. Indeed, a market society is likely to be characterized by a large number of such relationships. However, when we seek to apply these values at a societal level – by helping people of whom we do not have direct personal knowledge – the market mechanism becomes the most appropriate means of realizing such ends. Any attempt to organize society altruistically without recourse to market mechanisms will lead to economic and social disaster as the only means to efficiently allocate resources and ensure that the cost of the goods and services produced does not exceed the benefits derived is abandoned.

This positive account of the ethics of the market will now be developed in response to a number of objections that may be raised to the argument presented in this chapter: is the wealth generated by the market distributed equally or fairly? Are the contracts entered into in the market genuinely voluntary? Does the prosperity that the market creates actually enhance human well-being? Does the market undermine society's 'moral capital' by encouraging and rewarding the pursuit of self-interest? First, however, the next chapter will consider whether the prices generated by the market do indeed accurately reflect the needs of other people and the relative urgency of those needs as claimed in the account set out in this chapter.

3
Prices and Needs

The epistemological function of market prices is central to the ethical case for the market made in this book: it is claimed that within an advanced economy, price signals facilitate economic coordination more successfully and communicate the needs of people more accurately than any other mechanism.

An appreciation of the communicative function performed by prices within a market economy has long been part of mainstream economic theory. In the Walrasian tradition of classical economics it is accepted that prices provide information about the relative value of goods and services throughout an economy that enables individuals to learn the relative cost of different patterns of consumption. As Kreps (1988, p. 114) has described: 'the notion that prices contain and convey information is standard doctrine among economists'.

Despite the centrality of the informational properties of market prices to economic theory a number of scholars from outside and inside the discipline of economics have argued that an account of the role of market prices such as that set out in the previous chapter seriously overestimates the ability of market prices to accurately reflect people's needs and the resources available to satisfy those needs, and to efficiently guide dispersed economic actors to spontaneously coordinate their activities.

It has been argued that prices do not accurately reflect people's needs, but rather the purchasing power of different individuals based upon their income and wealth:

What [the market] responds to is 'effective demand,' that is, desires backed up by money or the willingness to pay for things...it means that the market does not respond to needs as such and does not draw any distinction between urgent needs and intense desires. (Anderson 1990, p. 183)

Furthermore, it is claimed that many important values simply cannot be represented as market prices without committing 'a fundamental conceptual error' because such non-economic values cannot be expressed in monetary terms (Keat 2000, p. 55).

It has also been claimed that prices do not convey the information necessary to enable economic actors to successfully coordinate their plans and, moreover, information alone is insufficient to bring about economic coordination:

Even given mutual knowledge of projected discoordination, no adjustment by any particular actor of his or her own actions will necessarily lead to coordination. There must be some mechanism whereby producers can mutually adjust plans in order that activities be coordinated. (O'Neill 1998, p. 137)

If prices do not perform the epistemological function that was claimed for them in the ethical account of the market presented in Chapter 2 then there must be an important role for government intervention in the economy to ameliorate the shortcomings of market prices, either by directly providing those goods and services that the market under-supplies because market prices do not communicate the demand for them or by deliberately bringing about economic coordination where the market has failed to do so. This chapter will show why these critiques of the epistemological function of the price mechanism are misplaced and demonstrate that market prices do indeed perform the function that was claimed for them in Chapter 2.

Plan of the chapter

This chapter will set out in detail the three principal objections to the view that market prices accurately reflect people's needs and are capable of guiding economic actors to successfully coordinate their actions: that prices do not reflect need, but rather the purchasing power of different individuals, which in turn reflects economic inequalities; that there are needs and values that cannot be categorized in monetary terms and to attempt to do so involves a fundamental misunderstanding of the nature of the thing so presented, and that recent advances in the field of the economics of information have questioned the informational efficiency of prices.

After presenting each of the above three objections to the ethical case for the market, this chapter will then present the counter-arguments. It will be shown that the first objection principally concerns questions of distributional justice rather than the epistemological function of market prices and that no price can reflect an 'objective' judgement about the moral worth of different goods and services – not least because such an objective judgement is impossible. In response to the second objection, it will be shown that the claim that certain values cannot be expressed in monetary terms is founded upon a misconception of the economic process. Finally, the chapter will argue that while recent scholarship examining the economics of information has focused attention on the need to clarify the exact role that prices perform, much recent work has misinterpreted the claims made for market prices and neglected the crucial importance of competition in the process of creative discovery necessary to achieving economic coordination.

Prices, need and purchasing power

Perhaps the most enduring and the most straightforward criticism of the claim that market prices accurately reflect people's needs and their relative urgency concerns the actual relative prices that exist in real world market economies. Observation of real world market economies shows that the prices of different goods and services often bear little relation to what many people would deem to be their true moral worth. As the Chicago economist Frank H. Knight (1997, p. 48) described:

> No one contends that a bottle of old wine is ethically worth as much as a barrel of flour, or a fantastic evening wrap for some potentate's mistress as much as a substantial dwelling-house, though such relative prices are not unusual.

Indeed, even more stark examples of the prices commanded by non-necessities than those provided by Knight can be cited. In May 1990, for example, Van Gogh's portrait *Dr Gachet* was sold at a New York auction house for $82 million, while today a luxury yacht has a multi-million pound price tag. It is difficult to contend that the need for these goods, their value or social utility, exceeds many times over that of essentials such as food, clothing and shelter, or adequate healthcare and sanitation in the poorest parts of the world.

It has been claimed, then, that prices and profits do not reflect the social value of a good or service, but rather the purchasing power of different individuals. As Knight (1997, p. 47) argued: 'The money value of a product is a matter of "demand", which in turn reflects the tastes and purchasing power of the buying public.' The fact that millionaires wish to buy luxury yachts means that profits can be made from their manufacture and supply, while little profit is to be made from feeding and clothing those who have little money. Hence, according to McMurtry (1997, p. 645), the only needs that the market satisfies are those that are backed by money:

> Under the rules of the free market, need without effective demand (i.e., the purchasing power of money) is not recognized. It counts for nothing. Need with no money to back it has no reality or value in the market.

It is argued that those who have the necessary financial resources will have their needs and wants satisfied, while those who do not have such purchasing power will go without. Market prices, it is alleged, do not discriminate between 'urgent needs and intense desires'; if money is available to support a particular want or desire, then the market will satisfy that demand irrespective of how deeply or urgently the need is felt (Anderson 1990).

It is contended that, contrary to the claims made in Chapter 2, market prices do not reflect the relative urgency of the needs for different goods and services. Rather it is said that prices reflect economic inequalities and, in particular, the ability of the wealthy to use their purchasing power to satisfy their demand for the consumption of luxury goods and services.

Prices as a 'category mistake'

A second objection to the claim that prices accurately reflect people's need for different goods and services concerns whether all human needs and values can be expressed as monetary prices. It has been argued that to attempt to conceptualize certain values and needs in terms of prices represents a 'category mistake': the use of a completely erroneous or inappropriate frame of reference to understand or categorize a particular phenomenon.

This critique of market prices is distinct from the claim made by Walzer (1983) and others that there should be moral limits to the goods and services that can be legitimately bought and sold in the marketplace. Rather, it is argued that even if we have no moral or philosophical objection to the pricing of particular goods, services and values, there are certain goods, services and values that *cannot practically be priced.*

A category mistake is said to occur when one concept is predicated of another that makes no sense in relation to it (Ryle 1949, 1953). As the environmental philosopher Mark Sagoff (1988, pp. 93–4) has described, to 'say that the square root of two is blue' represents a category mistake 'because colour concepts are not of a logical type that can meaningfully be predicated of numbers'. Similarly, to say that a sound is rigid, a chair feels tired, or that a car is laughing are all likewise absurd statements that constitute category mistakes.

According to Sagoff (1988, pp. 92–5), those preferences that are properly satisfied by private markets can be appropriately expressed as monetary prices. Relative preferences for ice cream as oppose to sorbet, for example, or for different models of television, are properly expressed as prices. People's moral and political values, however, cannot be expressed as prices without committing a category mistake because these values do not refer to desires or wants, but to deeper and more important normative beliefs.

In the context of environmental policy-making, for example, Sagoff has argued that it is not possible to attach a price to the deeper values that people attach to the unspoilt natural environment without making a category mistake. Hence, a Cost–Benefit Analysis that aims to calculate the cost of pollution may take into account factors such as the cost of cleaning a polluted river, but it is limited by the fact that the value that people place on the enjoyment of the natural environment simply cannot be expressed as a monetary price. Because such an analysis cannot take into account the intrinsic value people place on environmental conservation it will always underestimate the cost of pollution. Similarly, it has been argued that the depth of people's opposition to war is another example of a value that cannot be expressed in terms of relative prices because such opposition is based upon deeper moral and political values than the consumer preferences people express in the marketplace (Keat 2000, Chapter 3).

It is argued, then, that the epistemological power of prices is severely limited by the fact that certain values and beliefs cannot be communicated as market prices. Any decision-making process that is over-reliant on the informational properties of prices is therefore liable to marginalize those human values and beliefs that are in fact the most salient and deeply held. As such, it is argued that limits must be placed on the scope of the market so that those values that market processes cannot represent and communicate are not neglected or marginalized.

The informational efficiency of prices

Hayek (1948b, pp. 85–6) famously illustrated the coordinating properties of market prices with the example of a rise in the price of tin caused by its increased scarcity. If a new use for tin was discovered, or one of the sources of supply of tin was eliminated, the subsequent rise in its price would lead users to a number of different responses: some would introduce substitute factors of production, some might produce new goods that used less tin, others might be forced to raise the price of their goods produced using tin. The effect of the increased scarcity of tin would rapidly spread throughout the whole economy via the price mechanism and bring about a whole host of changes and adjustments, with very few market participants knowing, or needing to know, the actual cause of the change. The 'marvel' of the price mechanism, then, was that the dispersed actors within an economy could successfully adjust their plans to maintain economic coordination on the basis of *very little information*:

> It does not matter . . . *why* at the particular moment more screws of one size than of another are wanted, *why* paper bags are more readily available than canvas bags, or *why* skilled labour, or particular machine tools, have for the moment become more difficult to obtain. All that is significant . . . is *how much or less* difficult to procure they have become compared with other things. . . . (Hayek 1948b, p. 84)

The information that prices communicate is simultaneously extremely complex and extremely simple. In terms of complexity, prices communicate information that is beyond the comprehension of any single mind: prices reflect the subjective perceptions, and personal and tacit knowledge held by the myriad of different individuals dispersed throughout the economy. In terms of the simplicity of that information, prices ostensibly communicate only a series of relative numerical valuations: prices provide information of the value of different goods and services, but they do not inform us *why* a particular good or service is valued more highly than another.

It is this limited nature of the information that prices communicate that has led a number of scholars to question their informational efficiency. According to O'Neill (1998, p. 134), the key question is, 'does the information so communicated [by the price mechanism] in fact lead to the coordination of the activities of independent actors?' For O'Neill, it is questionable whether the price mechanism communicates sufficient information to ensure the coordination of individual actions and whether the communication of the relevant information is all that is necessary to ensure that individuals are able to coordinate their actions.

O'Neill's critique of the informational efficiency of prices is grounded in the work on the economics of information undertaken by Grossman and Stiglitz (1976, 1980). While accepting Hayek's basic premise that prices perform a crucial communicative function within a market economy, Grossman and Stiglitz nevertheless argued that prices do not communicate information in an optimal fashion. They argued that there are a number of instances where prices will not communicate all the information necessary for market transactions to attain an equilibrium position, or, conversely, that there are conditions where prices may convey too much information, which may lead to a breakdown of the operation of the relevant markets (Thomsen 1992).

Grossman and Stiglitz (1976) argued that prices may not communicate all the information necessary for market participants to respond effectively to changes in the marketplace because individuals may need to know more than that a price has risen or fallen. They may also need to know *why* a price has risen or fallen. In the case of Hayek's example of a rise in the price of tin, for instance, it may be very costly for a manufacturing firm that uses tin as a principal factor of production to replace tin in its production process, so before taking such a decision the firm will require more information than simply knowledge of a change in price. It may also need to know the reason for the price rise and how long the new price is likely to remain. Hence, as Grossman (1976, p. 585) commented, 'It is not enough for traders to observe only prices', successful adjustment within a market economy will require additional information. 'The price system', Grossman and Stiglitz (1976, p. 247) concluded, 'conveys some information, but does not transmit all the information from the informed to the uninformed.' Hence, it is argued that prices do not communicate all the relevant information necessary to achieve economic coordination.

Grossman and Stiglitz also argued that if prices did perform the function that Hayek ascribed to them, then they would convey too much information, leading to a breakdown of economic coordination. Here, Grossman and Stiglitz interpret Hayek's argument as claiming that prices communicate information that individuals have themselves collected at some personal cost. The price of a new children's toy, for example, may reflect market research undertaken at a producer's expense has. In a situation where prices communicate all available information, however, there is an incentive for individuals to stop gathering costly information and simply obtain information costlessly by observing the price signals generated by the market. As a consequence, prices will cease to communicate costly information, because such information will no longer be collected. According to Grossman (1976), when prices reveal too much information, as in the way Hayek is said to have described, a breakdown in the market will occur. The problem, then, is a market failure created by externalities and free-riding behaviour; where information is costly, uninformed individuals are able to free-ride on the information collected by others by simply observing the price signals generated by the market, creating a disincentive against the collection of that information necessary to a functioning price system.

O'Neill (1998, Chapter 10) has built upon the work of Grossman and Stiglitz to similarly argue that the market does not communicate sufficient information to ensure the successful coordination of individual plans. O'Neill has argued that the seeming communicative efficiency of the price mechanism in fact produces the cycles of boom and bust that Marx predicted would occur within capitalist economies. According to O'Neill, within a market economy, producers and consumers are reliant on the information communicated by the price mechanism, but this information is too basic to facilitate anything beyond a knee-jerk response to price fluctuations: when a change in price occurs, all producers within the economy respond in unison, either expanding or contracting production. Because the price mechanism does not communicate information about why a price has changed, or how long a change may last, it is argued that producers have little option but to respond to the bare fact of the price change, rather than to make a more measured response that would require better information. The problem is compounded by the fact that the competitive nature of a market economy is said to create a disincentive against the sharing and communication of information by other means. Firms that are rivals, it is argued, will withhold information that could be useful to their competitors, who must instead rely on the rudimentary information communicated by the price mechanism. The result is a series of over-corrections in response to price changes, creating a cycle of boom and bust.

According to O'Neill (1998, Chapter 10), the successful coordination of individual plans requires more than simply the information communicated by prices (or indeed information communicated by some other means). It is argued that economic coordination not only requires that individuals within an economy possess the relevant knowledge about the needs of others and the resources that might be utilized to meet those needs, it also requires the existence of a deliberate mechanism to secure coordination and mutual adjustment. Again, the competitive nature of a market economy is alleged to inhibit the attainment of optimum levels of mutual adjustment because in a competitive market economy it is in the interests of each firm that their competitors cease production. Hence, disincentives exist that inhibit the mutual adjustments of plans that would facilitate more effective coordination between firms. Instead, adjustments within the market occur via a series of painful shocks and dislocations when firms go bust as a result of a sudden movement of resources in response to a price fluctuation. It is claimed that only an economy organized cooperatively and subject to deliberate control can operate harmoniously:

> The solution [to the problem of economic coordination] lies in a cooperative economy with some mechanism for distributing

information that is relevant in order to coordinate plans, and a mechanism for mutual adjustment of plans given this information. It requires a mechanism that does the job that Hayek falsely claims the price mechanism performs. (O'Neill 1998, p. 138)

For O'Neill, the reliance of a market economy on the coordinating properties of the price mechanism means that such economies are inherently unstable, staggering through a cycle of boom and bust and prone to sudden shocks and dislocations that see large numbers of firms suddenly cease production, with the resultant human costs of unemployment and financial insecurity.

The three critiques of the epistemological function performed by market prices presented above all focus on the imperfections of the price mechanism and its alleged inability to accurately communicate information about the needs of the different individuals dispersed throughout that economy. While the price mechanism is by no means perfect, this chapter will now show why each of these critiques fails to provide a compelling counter-argument against the positive ethical case for the market set out in Chapter 2.

Purchasing power, prices and distribution

The differential purchasing power enjoyed by different individuals is reflected in the prices generated within a market economy. As Mises (1981, p. 490) described: 'The market is a democracy in which every penny gives a right to vote', but, 'the various individuals have not the same power to vote', because 'The richer man casts more ballots than the poorer fellow.' Similarly, Milton Friedman (1976, pp. 10–11) noted that in the economic democracy of the marketplace, 'voting is in proportion to the number of dollars a person has', a fact that 'is not obviously "just"'.

The price mechanism works because it communicates information about people's needs *and the resources available to meet those needs*; if the price mechanism did not reflect the purchasing power of different individuals it would not perform its epistemological function because it would not communicate information about the resources available to be put to different uses. An individual without resources in any economy – market or non-market – will be unable to satisfy their needs. For this reason, as will be discussed in more detail in the next chapter, there is a strong case for ensuring that each individual has the resources to satisfy their basic needs. People's basic needs can be satisfied in a non-market, subsistence economy, but the epistemological power of the price mechanism is relevant to an advanced economy able to attain a level of complexity and prosperity beyond a subsistence economy. It is once we seek to meet people's needs beyond the most basic requirements of food, clothing and shelter that the price mechanism becomes the most effective means of ascertaining people's needs and preferences and their relative urgency. This is because, as noted in the previous chapter, once we move beyond the most basic requirements, information about people's needs is dispersed throughout the economy, highly subjective and frequently tacit. Where there are a practically infinite number of alternative uses of our resources it is impossible to deliberately comprehend the relative urgency of so many different needs and preferences, yet the price mechanism spontaneously performs this feat.

It clearly is the case that many of the relative prices generated within a market economy do offend our sense of the moral worth of different goods and services. The fact that one bottle of wine may cost more than the monthly food bill for a family of four, or that a new sports car may command a higher price than a family house, can hardly be considered moral or just. It is impossible, however, to calculate or to determine an objectively 'correct' or 'just' price for any good or service because no good or service has a fixed value or utility; as every economics undergraduate knows, a glass of water has a very different marginal utility for a traveller lost in the desert and for a student seated in a lecture theatre.

Prices, in common with any other mechanism for ascertaining people's needs, can only reflect people's subjective perceptions of the relative urgency of their own needs, and it is not possible to state definitively that one of the finest vintages of wine really does have less value than the monthly food bill of an average family, or that a top of the range sports car really is worth less than an average family house. If one individual saved for ten years to purchase a bottle of one of the finest vintages of wine ever produced, would it really be the case that the price did not reflect its 'true' value – at least to that person? Hence, it cannot be said definitively that a deliberative process of allocating values to different goods and services would arrive at a different set of 'prices' to those allocated by the market.

There is no one objective or true value for any good or service against which to compare the prices generated in the marketplace. On the contrary, the value of every good and service can only be determined by consumer demand (and produces willingness to meet that demand) which will be driven by each individual's subjectively defined needs and preferences. While the price mechanism is not perfect, it is the most effective means of communicating information about people's needs yet discovered, so if we wish to help other people of whom we have no direct personal knowledge then the most efficacious way to do so is by responding to the price signals generated by the market.

Many of the objections to the relative prices generated by the market, such as those made by Anderson, Knight and McMurtry above, are in essence objections to the distribution of income and wealth within a market economy that enables some individuals to purchase luxury items while others do not have the means to do likewise. If it is believed that the prices generated by the market do not accurately reflect people's needs because of the distortions created by economic inequalities, this may lead to an argument for redistributing resources (questions of distribution will be considered in the next chapter), but it does not lead to an argument for abandoning the price mechanism, which would only plunge society into the economic darkness of a price-less economy.

Prices and values

The distinction drawn by Sagoff and others between those goods, services and values that can be properly expressed in terms of market prices and those that cannot is an effective and well-made critique of the kind of Cost–Benefit Analysis that has come to inform much contemporary environmental policy-making. The idea that politicians or bureaucrats can arbitrarily attach 'prices' to the value of different resources as a means of assessing the likely costs and benefits of different policies is indeed highly dubious. Only prices that have arisen heuristically from the exchange of property titles in the marketplace can accurately reflect the costs and benefits of different alternatives. There is no reason why any arbitrarily selected 'price' should accurately reflect, for example, the value that people attach to an unpolluted river or the cost of the development of a piece of unspoilt wilderness.

This critique of non-market prices should not, however, be extended to prices that have genuinely arisen in the marketplace. There is no *a priori* reason why market prices should be able to communicate some values but not others because in reality, as Sowell (1996, p. 79) has described, there is no dichotomy between monetary or economic values and non-monetary or non-economic values: 'there are only noneconomic values'. Money and prices are simply proxy measures of the *non-economic* values that inform the choices that all individuals must make on a daily basis: prices simply provide a means of representing the *non-economic* trade-offs inherent in any decision.

Hence, if a local amenity group who owned the development rights to a piece of unspoilt wilderness were to turn down an offer of a million pounds from a developer wishing to build a factory on the land, that decision would demonstrate that their valuation of the unspoilt land exceeded one million pounds. Similarly, if the same group accepted an offer of two million pounds from another developer then that decision would show that their valuation of the unspoilt land did not exceed two million pounds. There is absolutely no reason why the value of an environmental resource should not be expressed in these terms.

Indeed, there is good reason to believe that people's values and preferences should be expressed in monetary terms because relative prices reflect the fact that every choice involves trade-offs against other alternatives. Where resources are finite, including resources of time and energy, the decision to devote resources to one particular use means that those resources cannot be employed elsewhere:

> Prices are important not because money is considered paramount but because prices are a fast and effective conveyor of information through a vast society in which fragmented knowledge must be coordinated. To say that we 'cannot put a price' on this or that is to misconceive the economic process. Things cost because other things could have been produced with the same time, effort and material. (Sowell 1996, p. 80)

In the context of environmental conservation, prices reflect the fact that preservation of the environment will produce benefits, such as the enjoyment of the natural environment and the survival of wildlife, but it will also involve costs: land may not be developed; goods and services may not be produced or may be produced more expensively in a different location or by different means; people may not be employed or may have to move to find employment in a different location. To suggest that prices should not be attached to environmental resources is to negate the fact that conservation involves benefits *and costs*.

Prices, then, communicate the fact that such alternatives are not costless and by so doing prices enable people to decide whether the benefits of different courses of action do indeed outweigh the costs. Prices provide an objective representation of subjective costs and choices: it is possible to add up a balance sheet of prices whereas it is impossible to quantify the subjective costs and choices that inform those prices in the same way (Buchanan 1999; Pasour 1978).

As noted above, prices have important advantages over other means of communicating an individual's values and preferences. In the present context it should first be noted that prices are a 'universal language' that can be easily understood by all and is rarely subject to misinterpretation. Prices are able to communicate information across the world between people who have never met in person and could not communicate directly if they ever did meet face to face.

Second, prices communicate information that would not exist if it were not generated in the marketplace. Where the higher demand for one good over another results in a higher price for that popular good, information is communicated that would not exist if the market process did not take place. The information communicated by the price mechanism often contains tacit knowledge that can only be expressed in the act of choosing and therefore cannot be communicated verbally.

Third, in order for the price mechanism to perform its epistemological function, market participants are not required to comprehend anything beyond their own self-interest, and even this may be an extremely basic comprehension. Whereas decisions reached by conscious deliberation depend upon the quality and quantity of information utilized by participants in the decision-making process, the price mechanism functions regardless of the epistemological shortcomings of market participants. For individuals to learn about the needs and values of others in the marketplace they need do nothing more than pursue their own self-interest under the guidance of the price signals generated by the market (Meadowcroft 2002; Pennington 2003a).

Fourth, the choices that people make in the marketplace are costed against the alternatives. Whereas in the political realm choices may often appear costless (or at the very least the costs are likely to be highly dispersed), in the marketplace to purchase a good or service means that other alternatives must be foregone. For this reason choices made in the marketplace are more likely to be indicative of genuine preferences and values rather than being a wish list based upon the seemingly costless alternatives that people vote for in the context of democratic decision-making (Pennington 2003b).

The failure of the political process as a mechanism for communicating people's true preferences may be illustrated by the high levels of government spending on 'defence' in most liberal democracies, even during periods when the threat of external aggression or terrorism has been minimal. Democratically elected politicians of all ideological persuasions have been willing to divert sizeable resources to the military, yet it may be contended that if every individual member of society was personally given the choice as to whether the whole of their personal contribution to the defence budget should be spent on the military or at least some of it devoted to other alternatives, such as their children's education or improved healthcare, it is unlikely that the armed forces would receive such large budget allocations. Hence, if the mechanism for allocating the budget for national defence was taken out of the political realm and put into the economic realm, it is likely that people's genuine preferences would be translated into reduced funding for the military. Indeed, the contention that the political process communicates people's preferences for peace over war more effectively than the market process would seem to defy the evidence of the propensity of liberal democratic (and other) states around the world to engage in military action.

It is not the case, then, that there are certain values that cannot be expressed in monetary terms without committing a category mistake. On the contrary, the value that we attach to the unspoilt natural environment, our preferences for peace over war, or simply an individual's desire to eat a diet free from meat, can all be translated into a market context. Indeed, it has been shown there is good reason to suppose that the market may be more successful at communicating our deepest-held values than the political process. While prices are not a perfect mechanism for expressing all preferences and values, prices heuristically determined in the marketplace nevertheless communicate information about the trade-offs inherent in alternative courses of action more successfully than any other means. Given that choices must be made between competing alternatives, market prices provide the best possible representation of the subjective pecuniary and non-pecuniary costs and benefits inherent in such decisions.

Prices, information and coordination

Grossman and Stiglitz's critique of the epistemological efficacy of the price mechanism – that also forms the basis of O'Neill's critique – is based upon a partial misinterpretation of Hayek's conception of the role performed by prices and the nature of the information communicated by prices. Grossman and Stiglitz, working within the context of neo-classical equilibrium theory which models markets as operating under conditions of perfect information, interpret Hayek within that same framework to be claiming that prices communicate all the information necessary for markets to attain a Pareto Optimal equilibrium position where one person cannot be made better-off without another being made worse-off. Hence, Grossman and Stiglitz understand Hayek to be arguing that prices act as 'sufficient statistics', that they communicate all the available information that is already known to market participants and by so doing facilitate economic coordination (Boettke 1997; Thomsen 1992).

In order to address this criticism it is necessary to present a slightly more sophisticated view of the epistemological function performed by market prices than was necessary in the previous chapter. Hayek's argument centres on the role performed by prices in facilitating economic coordination in conditions of *disequilibrium*. It is not contended that prices facilitate the creation of perfectly competitive markets in constant states of equilibrium by perfectly communicating all available and relevant information, but that prices facilitate a process of inter-subjective learning in which the presence of profit opportunities provide incentives for producers and consumers to discover new prices and new courses of action. It is because prices are *imperfect* that they facilitate the entrepreneurial activity that leads to the creative discovery of new ways of doing things. A price based upon producers' subjective perceptions of consumer demand, for example, may be set higher than the price most consumers are willing to pay for a particular product, thus providing the opportunity for a new entrant to the market to entrepreneurially supply the good at a lower price.

It is the very fact that prices do not communicate all the relevant information that provides the opportunity for entrepreneurial activity crucial to the Hayekian view of the market process. As Garrison (1985, p. 132) has described, in Hayek's (1948b, p. 85) example of the impact of a rise in the price of tin it was not claimed that the *only* information necessary for adjustment to take place is knowledge of the price change, but that *the great majority* of tin users do not need to know why the price has risen so long as '*some of them know directly* of the new demand, and switch resources over to it' [emphasis added to Hayek's original by Garrison].

A rise in the price of tin, then, will produce a chain of different reactions among producers and consumers. One manufacturer may pay more for this particular factor of production and pass on the extra cost to the consumer; some consumers may then decide to switch to cheaper products that do not use tin, others may find that the price rise is not significant enough to alter their relative preferences. Another manufacturer may seek more information from their supplier as to the reason for the change in price before responding; another may simply decide to replace tin with aluminium in the production process. Hayek's point, then, was not that the change in the price of tin brought about a uniform reaction throughout the marketplace that resulted in an instantaneous correction and a return to equilibrium, but that the price change communicated information that provoked a series of reactions, some of which may accurately interpret or anticipate present and future market conditions, while others may be based upon erroneous inferences from the price change. The plurality of responses leads to a process of heuristic learning in which new possibilities are discovered and acted upon.

Economic actors do not respond in an objective and predictable manner to an objective body of knowledge communicated by prices, but interpret essentially subjective knowledge through their own subjective filters. The price mechanism is irreplaceable because it is able to communicate incomplete and imperfect information.

Hayek's argument, then, was that prices acted as 'surrogate' rather than 'sufficient' statistics. Prices are one means via which information is communicated within a market economy, but prices cannot be the only source of information, because this would create a non-sensical situation where there would not be any information for prices to communicate. As Garrison (1985, p. 133) concluded:

> Hayek called our attention to the marvel of the market economy functioning as it does on the basis of so little knowledge; he did not insist on a miracle in which the economy functions in the total absence of knowledge.

Furthermore, Grossman and Stiglitz are wrong to assume that prices principally communicate information that has been collected at some cost to the collector, so that if prices work effectively such information will cease to be collected and the market process will breakdown. In fact, the essence of the epistemological function of market prices is that they communicate people's subjective and frequently tacit preferences, information that could not be collected by any other means, such as via market research. While the prices set by producers may often reflect market research that they have under-taken or their judgements about consumer demand, the prices that consumers are willing to pay for goods and services will communicate costless information about their preferences that could not be collected by any other means. Even if all firms simultaneously ceased to collect costly information, the price mechanism would still communicate abundant information generated by the actions of consumers, ensuring the continued operation of the market.

Grossman and Stiglitz's work on the efficiency of prices has undoubtedly performed an important function in drawing attention to possible ambiguities in Hayek's original scholarship. This has led more recent scholars to revisit Hayek's original work and clarify the exact function it is claimed prices perform. Recent work by Garrison (1985), Kirzner (1992, 2000) and Thomsen (1992) has shown that once Hayek's insights are properly situated outside the narrow confines of neo-classical equilibrium theory his work retains its original authority.

O'Neill has similarly misinterpreted Hayek's claim that market prices are the most effective means of communicating certain economic information to mean that Hayek believes that prices are the only source of information necessary to produce mutual adjustments in a market economy. In reality, the Hayekian position is that while many changes in production or consumption will result from price fluctuations, others will come about in response to information received from other sources. A firm may reduce output because of a fall in the number of orders it has received, for example, or in response to press reports of a pending rise in production costs. These changes will, of course, then be reflected in price movements.

Equally, O'Neill is wrong to assume that all producers and consumers will respond to a price signal in a uniform manner. As noted above, every price signal must pass through the filter of each individual's subjective perceptions, which will be informed by highly personal knowledge that will lead to a number of different reactions. The rivalrous nature of a market economy will also mean that producers will actively seek opportunities to second-guess and out-manoeuvre each other, rather than automatically responding in the same way. It should also be noted that – contra O'Neill's depiction of a market economy – not all firms in a market economy are competitors: many will engage in long-term cooperative relationship as suppliers and subcontractors (see, for example, Lorenz 1988).

In a market economy even rivalrous firms cannot avoid communicating information via prices, their own advertising or their own production decisions. It is impossible to keep secret, for example, the launch of a new product or the construction of a new factory. Moreover, O'Neill's argument neglects the crucial role performed by competition in *discovering* the information necessary for economic coordination, such as the most appropriate levels of production of different goods and services. The idea that non-competitive firms could cooperatively decide the most socially beneficial use of the resources at their disposal is simply another example of the synoptic delusion that one omnipotent mind or group of minds working together can comprehend the economy in its totality and plan outcomes accordingly. As Steele (1992, p. 251) noted in a response to an earlier version of O'Neill's argument: 'even if all the production plans were known, it would still *not* be known a. what the desirable total output would be, nor b. what the best division of output among those firms would be'.

Competition within a market economy is not simply an unfortunate by-product of the market process that inhibits economic coordination and development: competition is essential to the heuristic learning essential to any successful economy. Just as the most effective tactical formation for a football team can be discovered only through the competitive test of playing matches that generates new information about the success or failure of different tactics, so economic knowledge, such as the most desirable total output of different goods and services, can be discovered only via the process of competition in the marketplace in which different firms compete to discover what consumers want and then satisfy those needs and preferences (Hayek 1978).

It is not the case that reliance on the communicative function of the price mechanism within a market economy leads to a series of booms and slumps or that adjustment can only occur via severe shocks that see large numbers of firms go bankrupt. On the contrary, while bankruptcies and recessions do, of course, occur in market economies, the empirical evidence of the functioning of real world market economies demonstrates remarkable levels of stability and subtly in adjustments, leading to sustained economic growth over many decades. As Steele (1992, p. 249) described, O'Neill's theory 'proves too much', because if it were accurate it would be the case 'that markets were frequently in severe crisis', yet, in reality, 'millions of market adjustments are made every day, smoothly and harmoniously, without a trace of "crisis"'. O'Neill's critique of the market is not supported by empirical evidence of inherent failings within market economies that result from their reliance on market prices as their principal coordinating mechanism.

Conclusion

Market prices do not reflect the objective moral worth of any good or service because no good or service has an objective moral worth. Rather, the value of any good or service can be determined only by the interplay of the subjective perceptions and preferences of individual consumers and producers in the marketplace. Prices reflect at what cost consumers are willing to purchase a good or service and at what cost producers are willing to supply it. Market prices establish and communicate this information more effectively than any other means.

Market prices do reflect the differential purchasing power of different individuals: because some wealthy people are willing to pay millions of pounds for a luxury yacht, producers will supply luxury yachts, while simultaneously many more people must ration many of life's simpler pleasures such as dining out or going to the cinema. The fact that prices reflect the differential purchasing power of different individuals is indicative of the epistemological power of the price mechanism: it efficiently communicates information about people's needs and the resources that may be used to meet those needs. Moral objections to the relative prices that exist in real world market economies are in effect objections to the distribution of income and wealth within these economies and as such they will be addressed in the next chapter. The most that such an objection can prove, however, is that the distribution of income and wealth within a market economy is unfair or unjust; even if this were the case it would not undermine the epistemological efficacy of the price mechanism but rather would constitute an argument for redistribution.

Market prices are a highly effective means of realizing and expressing all of people's values and preferences. Indeed, there is good reason to believe that market prices are a more effective means of communicating people's most deeply held preferences and values than the political process: market prices are a universal language that reflects dispersed, subjective and tacit knowledge; choices made in the marketplace are costed relative to the possible alternatives, and whereas the political process can only utilize knowledge that can be verbally articulated and intellectually comprehended by political actors, the market utilizes more knowledge than any single individual or group of people working together could possibly comprehend.

Recent scholarship on the economics of information that criticized Hayek's work on the epistemological function of market prices has misinterpreted the role assigned to prices in the Hayekian view of the market. Hayek did not view prices as the only sources of information necessary to secure coordination in a market economy, nor did he contend that prices communicated the perfect information required to achieve a state of Pareto Optimal equilibrium. On the contrary, Hayek stressed the role of disequilibrium prices as incomplete sources of information that facilitated a process of creative discovery and heuristic learning that enabled individuals to learn from the mistakes of the past and the present. Economic coordination did not arise from an imagined state of perfect equilibrium where every economic actor possessed perfect information perfectly communicated by prices, but resulted from a dynamic process of trial-and-error learning punctuated by innovation, mistakes and entrepreneurial discovery.

While market prices are not perfect, this chapter has shown that they nevertheless do perform the epistemological function attributed to them in Chapter 2. There is no perfect means of ascertaining people's needs and the resources available to meet those needs while simultaneously coordinating the activities of a myriad of dispersed economic actors, but market prices do enable people to meet the needs of others of whom they have no personal knowledge more effectively than any other means and enable market participants to spontaneously coordinate their actions. The next chapter will address the important questions relating to distributional justice in a market economy that were raised in this chapter in relation to purchasing power and are central to an evaluation of the ethics of the market.

4
Distribution and Justice

While it may be accepted that a market economy generates a level of prosperity that no other economic system can match, as noted in the previous chapter ethical objections may be raised as to how that wealth is distributed. It is undoubtedly the case that the unprecedented material wealth that a market economy produces is distributed unequally. The market will produce multi-millionaires such as Microsoft founder Bill Gates and Rolling Stones frontman Mick Jagger who are able to enjoy a lifestyle that the great majority of their contemporaries will never attain.

Critiques of distributional justice within the market have focused on the origins, the extent and the human consequences of these inequalities to argue that limits should be placed upon the extent to which the distribution of income and wealth is determined by the unfettered operation of market forces:

> Given the degree of inequality which will naturally arise from free market exchange, and the fact that these will be influenced by morally arbitrary factors such as natural endowment, fortunate upbringing, and just sheer luck it is important to work out some consensual view about where appropriate limits lie for an institution which embodies these features. (Plant 1992, p. 120)

It is claimed that the inequalities that naturally arise as a result of market exchanges are unjust and could become so extreme that one section of society could be condemned to poverty while the rest enjoy prosperity; while a market economy might create national prosperity, the cost of that prosperity may be the 'social exclusion' of those who are condemned to a life of poverty at the bottom of the economic ladder (for example, Byrne 1997).

It is contended that 'social justice' need not require the complete eradication of economic inequality, but rather the limitation of inequalities to an acceptable level. According to Miller (2001, p. 243):

> [I]n a market economy it will almost certainly be inevitable, and be regarded as fair, that there should be income differentials within firms. But there seem to be no reasons, either of economic necessity or of fairness, for these differentials to be anywhere near as large as they are now in most capitalist systems.

For Miller, it is 'fair for the managing director of a large company to be paid not more than, say, three or four times the wage of an unskilled worker, with proportionate differentials in between'. Similarly, Galbraith (2002) has argued that a proper goal of public policy is to attain '*sufficient* equality in the distribution of income' [original emphasis] via redistributive taxation.

It is argued, then, that it is an appropriate role of the state to *limit* the extent to which the distribution of income and wealth are determined by market forces, rather than to create strict equality of economic outcomes or to replace the market in its entirety.

At first sight, distributional justice would appear to be one ethical criterion where the market must be found wanting, given that it is the case that market forces produce inequalities of income and wealth that bear no relation to need.

However, this chapter will show that even though the unequal distribution of income and wealth produced by a market economy bears no relation to need or desert, and is not combined with equality of opportunity, it should nevertheless be considered just because it meets the only relevant moral criterion: procedural justice. Moreover, the unequal rewards that people receive from their participation in the market reflect the value of their economic contributions as determined by the subjective perceptions of consumers and producers in the marketplace and are an essential part of the prosperity created by the market that benefits all members of society. It will also be argued, however, that the state should guarantee every citizen a basic minimum income to ensure that no one be subject of destitution or absolute poverty for whatever reason.

Plan of the chapter

This chapter will begin by setting out Nozick's entitlement theory of justice that shows that wherever people engage in voluntary exchanges inequalities of income and wealth will result. It will then consider the relationship of the outcomes produced by the market to desert and moral merit. Next, the chapter will show that the economic inequalities produced by the market are essential to the wealth creation that provides the only means of lifting large numbers of people out of poverty. For this reason the inequalities produced by the market can be said to benefit the least advantaged and the least well-off. Furthermore, while the inequalities produced by the market are not combined with equality of opportunity, they are nevertheless indicative of dynamic societies with high levels of economic mobility. Finally, it will be argued that while it is empirically the case that the prosperity generated by the market has effectively banished absolute poverty from contemporary capitalist societies, the state should nevertheless guarantee every citizen a minimum income to ensure that no one should be without the means of their own subsistence for any reason.

Justice, distribution and entitlement

The very concept of 'distributional justice' would appear to imply a conscious mechanism for the distribution of society's resources that may or may not have produced a just outcome, when, in reality, the distribution of resources within a market economy is the spontaneous by-product of a myriad of polycentric individual actions: the outcomes produced by the market are 'the results of human action but not of human design' (Hayek 1967a). The distribution of resources in a market economy does not result from one individual or group of individuals deciding who should get what. Rather, it arises spontaneously as a result of the voluntary actions of individual men and women, none of whom can fully comprehend the whole of which they are a part.

Probably the most famous and enduring description of the way in which income and wealth are distributed via a series voluntary exchanges is Robert Nozick's (1974, pp. 160–4) account of the wealth acquired by the basketball player Wilt Chamberlain in a fictional scenario in his classic of libertarian philosophy *Anarchy, State, and Utopia*. Taking as a starting point a distribution of resources that is considered just, which Nozick names D1, Nozick supposes that large numbers of people pay twenty-five cents directly to Wilt Chamberlain (in addition to the standard ticket price) in order to watch him play basketball. Supposing that one million people come through the turnstiles during the course of a season, Wilt Chamberlain would acquire additional personal wealth of $250,000: one individual has amassed a sizeable personal fortune as a consequence of many small and seemingly inconsequential exchanges. As a result of the voluntary actions of a million basketball fans and Wilt Chamberlain, a new distribution of resources has emerged, which Nozick names D2.

For Nozick, the new distribution of resources (D2) must be considered just because it meets the criteria of 'justice in acquisition' and 'justice in transfer'. The theoretical starting point of Nozick's example was a distribution of resources that was considered just (it is left to the reader to imagine what such a distribution might be) and then people voluntarily transferred their justly held resources to Chamberlain in return for a service (watching him play) that they considered more valuable than the twenty-five cents each paid. In neither case can an injustice be said to have occurred, therefore the outcome of the transactions described must logically be considered just:

> If D1 was a just distribution, and people voluntarily moved from it to D2, transferring parts of their shares they were given under D1 (what was it for if not to do something with?), isn't D2 also just? If the people were entitled to dispose of the resources to which they were entitled (under D1), didn't this also include their being entitled to give it to, or exchange it with, Wilt Chamberlain? (Nozick 1974, p. 161)

Nozick's example of Wilt Chamberlain's acquisition of wealth illustrates how 'liberty upsets patterns [of distribution]' and inevitably produces inequalities (Nozick 1974, p. 160; see also Hayek 1960, p. 85). Where people are allowed to make free choices as to how they use their resources, deviations from any preferred pattern of distribution will inevitably arise. Where a musician releases a record that is purchased by a large number of fans, where a firm poaches an employee from a rival with a large salary, or even where people enter a lottery with only one jackpot winner, inequalities of income and wealth will emerge.

For Nozick, justice in the distribution of resources can only be procedural. Because a distribution of resources is (or should be) the unintended consequence of the spontaneous actions of individual men and women, the only criterion of justice that is applicable is that the procedures that governed the steps that led to a particular distribution were just. The distribution of resources itself cannot be considered just or unjust, just as the outcome of a football match or the distribution of sexual partners likewise cannot be considered just or unjust; the only ethical consideration is whether the laws of the game were observed or whether the people who engaged in sexual acts consented.

Nozick's argument is a particularly devastating critique of those who would advocate the imposition of a particular pattern of distribution upon a society because it demonstrates that any preferred pattern of distribution can only be sustained either by outlawing voluntary exchanges between consenting adults or by seizing the resources that they have justly acquired in those voluntary exchanges. Neither course of action can be taken without creating an injustice by violating each individual's freedom to engage in voluntary exchanges or confiscating their justly acquired resources. Hence, Nozick (1974, p. 163) writes that 'no end-state principle or distributional patterned principle of justice can be continuously realized without continuous interference with people's lives'.

Nozick's critique of patterned theories of distribution has been so successful that even one of the most influential socialist egalitarian philosophers of the twentieth century, G. A. Cohen, has written that in the context of Nozick's entitlement theory, 'I think socialists do well to concede that an egalitarian principle should not be the only guide to the justice of holdings, or that, if it is, then justice should not be the only guide to policy with respect to holdings' (Cohen 1995, p. 25). Nozick's work highlighted the ease with which relatively large deviations from a preferred pattern of distribution will arise and hence the scale of tyranny that would be required to maintain a particular distribution of income and wealth, if not the practical impossibility of doing so. While the power of Nozick's thesis has produced Cohen's important concession, demonstrating the theoretical power of Nozick's argument as an abstract defence of distribution via the market, the application of Nozick's thesis to real world market economies may be more problematic.

Contemporary capitalism, private property and justice in acquisition

Nozick's entitlement theory is predicated upon exchanges that arise from an initial allocation of resources that is considered just. While this provides a theoretically robust refutation of the idea that a particular pattern of distribution can be sustained without violating the rights of individuals to engage in voluntary exchanges, it is less clear that this provides a successful defence of the distribution of resources in a real world market economy, given that many scholars would contend that the private property that individuals exchange in contemporary capitalist economies was not originally acquired according to the principle of justice in acquisition. It is argued that the private property rights that exist in capitalist societies simply provide a cloak of legal respectability to the possession of resources that were originally seized by occupation, violence and robbery (for example, Christman 1986; Phillips 1999, p. 63; Ryan 1981).

As noted in Chapter 2, liberal theories of property rights from which the Nozickian position is derived originate in Locke's (1993, Chapter 5) classic account of the origins of private property. For Locke, a property right was established when a person applied their labour to a natural resource in the state of nature: when an individual picked fruit from a tree, killed a buffalo or cleared and enclosed common land, that fruit, meat or land became that individual's property. Because each individual had a property right in their own person, when the labour of their body was mixed with the natural products of the earth, the result legitimately became their property. Locke further stipulated the proviso that it was not legitimate for an individual to take into private ownership so much of a given resource that there was none left for others to use or what had been captured would spoil.

Locke's theory of just acquisition was based upon a prescient appreciation of the rights of individuals to enjoy the fruits of their labour and of the collective benefits that arise from the institution of private property. Locke (1993, p. 291) stated that it was essential for the betterment of mankind that 'the Industrious and Rational' were able to cultivate and improve the land without 'the Fancy or Covetousness of the Quarrelsom and Contentious' free-riding upon or spoiling their work. Corn would not be grown on land where any person was free to take what they wanted, for example, but where land was privately owned corn would be grown in abundance. If the wastelands remained wild and open to all, in the absence of proper improvement and husbandry, a thousand acres would yield less produce than ten acres of well-cultivated land. Locke (1993, pp. 291–4) understood that industry, progress and a peaceful collective life all demanded that private property rights be established. Certainly there is compelling contemporary evidence that sustained economic growth cannot take place in the absence of a system of secure private property rights (for example, Soto 2000).

It has been argued, however, that Locke's theory of just acquisition was in reality intended to provide a moral and legal justification for the European feudal order and, in particular, for the European colonization of North America (for example, Arneil 1996). It is certainly the case, as Mises (1981, p. 32) has described, that, 'All ownership derives from occupation and violence.' That is, if we trace the origin of any private property to its original acquisition there will most likely come a point where that property was occupied or seized by force. The great majority of property rights in Europe owe their origins to medieval conflicts arising out of occupations and counter-occupations. Similarly, while some of the property acquired by the European colonialists in North America can be considered to have been justly acquired in that it was purchased fairly from the Native Americans or was genuine virgin territory, much of the land the colonialists acquired was in effect stolen from the Native Americans whose prior claim to the land was not recognized by the Europeans, particularly the English who conveniently decreed that only the English monarch could grant property titles (Watner 1983).

It is, of course, inevitable that the transition from (what might be termed) a 'pre-legal society' into a society governed by the rule of law involves the codification of those arrangements that existed prior to the rule of law. As Mises (1981, p. 35) described: 'In complaining that Law is nothing more or less than legalized injustice, one fails to perceive that it could only be otherwise if it had existed from the very beginning', so that, 'To demand that Law should have arisen legally is to demand the impossible.' Hence, the property rights that happen to exist when the rule of law is established are inevitably those that are enshrined into law, irrespective of the justice of their appropriation. This is not the result of a conscious decision on the part of those who hold the relevant property rights, but rather the inevitable result of a process of spontaneous and gradual evolution.

To argue that property rights are not justly held because they have their ultimate origins in a pre-legal social order characterized by occupation and violence is a complete *non-sequitur* because any form of property rights (even collective or socialist property rights) must involve a similar transition from non-legal to legal status, from a state where property rights were consistently challenged and subject to transfer by force, to one where property rights are respected and only subject to transfer by legal means.

Furthermore, as Nozick (1974, p. 178) has described, those who argue that private property rights involve the illegitimate appropriation of collective resources must also provide a theory of how such collective property rights arise: 'they must show why the persons living [in an area jointly] have rights to determine what is done with the land and resources there that persons living elsewhere don't have (with regard to the same land and resources)'. It is unclear how such arguments can be successfully made without recourse to the principles underpinning private property rights.

Similarly, the (in many cases well-founded) complaints that European colonialists stole land from Native Americans also implies that the Native Americans held a property right to the land that must also be based upon something approximate to a Lockean conception of just acquisition. Lyons (1981, p. 355), for example, has described the European conquest of America as involving the 'monumental theft of land', clearly implying that the Native Americans held a property right over the land that was unjustly appropriated by the Europeans.

The fact that many of the private property rights that exist in contemporary capitalist societies cannot be traced back to acquisition in accordance with the principle of justice in acquisition does not diminish the success of Nozick's entitlement theory as a critique of patterned theories of distribution. It may mean, however, that Nozick's argument would logically justify rectification or compensation where it can be shown that private property rights were acquired unjustly, for example in the cases of the European conquest of American or Australia. In most contemporary market economies, however, the origins of the private property rights that exist are untraceable and any attempt to remedy the wrongs of the past would simply heap injustice upon injustice, on top of the dire social and economic consequences that follow where long-established private property rights are not respected by government. Where the rule of law and private property rights have been long-established (to the extent that their origins are no longer clear or they have passed through innumerable owners) then a situation tantamount to the justice in acquisition that Nozick described can be said to exist.

Exchange, distribution and consent

A second important critique of Nozick's entitlement theory concerns the claim that because no injustice has occurred in the process of moving from distribution D1 to distribution D2, it does not necessarily follow that the new distribution is itself just or has popular consent.

It has been argued that Nozick's entitlement theory is founded upon the questionable assumption that people value increasing their personal holdings more than they would value living in an egalitarian society; under distribution D1, people might be so committed to this particular pattern of distribution that they may choose not to engage in voluntary transactions so as not to disrupt it. According to Wolff (1991, p. 82): 'Individuals may well see ways of improving their particular share through voluntary transactions, but nevertheless refrain from taking them as they do not wish to disrupt equality.' Similarly, Cohen (1995, p. 29) has argued that Nozick's contention that liberty upsets patterns is founded upon 'the unargued premise' that 'citizens will want to perform capitalist acts'. Nozick's theory is said to rely upon unproven and tenuous assumptions about human nature, namely that people will choose to enhance their personal holdings rather than act in accordance with egalitarian principles.

Moreover, it is argued that those citizens who do engage in voluntary exchanges do not necessarily consent to the new distribution of resources that is produced as a result. Cohen (1995, Chapter 1) has argued that with the benefit of hindsight, people may judge that the distribution of resources resulting from a series of voluntary exchanges is unjust because of the externalities that arise as a consequence and because of its impact on people who did not participate in (and therefore consent to) the exchanges, notably those children who will inherit a distribution of income and wealth that may hinder their life chances.

In the case of Wilt Chamberlain, for example, the spectators who paid twenty-five cents to watch him play basketball may realize after the event that they have not only allocated Chamberlain a large sum of money, they have also unwittingly conferred upon him a large amount of power:

> For, once Chamberlain has received the payments, he is in a very special position of power in what was previously an egalitarian society. The fans' access to resources might now be prejudiced by the disproportionate access Chamberlain's wealth gives him, and the consequent power over others he now has. (Cohen 1995, p. 25)

An externality of economic exchanges is said to be the conferment of power upon those individuals who gain greater material resources than others as a result. According to Cohen (1995, p. 28), 'holdings are not only sources of enjoyment but, in certain distributions, sources of power', and in distribution D2, Chamberlain possesses 'considerable power... over others'. For this reason, it is argued that the justice of a particular distribution of resources not only depends upon how it was attained, but also upon the power relationships that it produces. Hence political authority may be legitimately used to maintain wealth differentials within 'acceptable levels' (Cohen 1995, p. 26).

The claim that people might willingly forgo economic exchanges so as to preserve a particular pattern of distribution neglects the fact that any economy advanced beyond a subsistence level must be founded upon a division of labour that must in turn be founded upon the exchange of goods and services. Unless every individual or family unit is completely self-sufficient, people have to engage in economic exchanges. Those who engage in economic exchanges need not seek to increase their holdings in order for inequalities to emerge. It is the repetition of mutually advantageous exchanges throughout an economy – the exchange of a good or service that one individual values less highly for a good or service that they value more highly – that cumulatively produces inequalities. Moreover, inequalities of income and wealth will not only arise as a result of exchanges, but also through resources being put to productive use or left to spoil. If every person was given an equal allocation of land, for example, the fact that some people were better gardeners than others or devoted more time to cultivation would mean that over time some people would accrue more resources than others even without any exchanges taking place (Mack 2002, p. 83). Nozick's contention that people will engage in activities that will upset a particular pattern of distribution is not an assumption about human nature but a straightforward empirical observation about the nature of an advanced economy.

In fact Cohen's critique of Nozick is itself founded upon two erroneous assumptions. First, although Cohen does not challenge or question the fact that the distribution of income and wealth produced by the market is not the result of deliberate design, he nevertheless assumes that the outcome of such a spontaneous and procedurally just process can itself be judged against a separate criterion of justice. As noted above, this is tantamount to assessing justice in the distribution of sexual partners or in the outcomes of football matches, where it similarly cannot be said to be just or unjust that a particular team won a particular football match – only that the game was played by the rules – or that a particular couple engaged in sexual acts while other people were left without partners – only that both parties freely choose to engage in such activity.

Howarth (1994) has criticized the Nozickian depiction of market exchange as an example of the 'reducibility thesis' in which the workings of a market economy are reduced to a series of simple, bilateral exchanges, but he does not offer an alternative account of how the market operates, other than to state that 'bilateral exchanges between consenting individuals normally *do* have far-reaching, and often deleterious, consequences for third parties not directly involved' (Howarth 1994, p. 17). The fact that the actions of individuals may have consequences for third parties does not alter the nature of the acts that those individuals engage in. The fact that one individual's relationship with their partner denies others the opportunity of a similar involvement does not alter the fact that their relationship is bilateral nor does it give others the right to veto it. Similarly, the fact that a football team may be relegated as a consequence of the result of a match between two other teams does not alter the fact that that match is a contest between those two teams alone nor does it give the players of the relegation threatened team the right to take to the pitch to try to influence the outcome. Nozick's 'reducibility thesis' is actually an accurate description of the relationships and exchanges that constitute a market economy and claiming otherwise does not alter this basic fact.

Second, Cohen assumes that the inequalities produced by a spontaneous and procedurally just distribution of income and wealth are undesirable or harmful to some individuals. Later sections of this chapter will show at length why this is not the case, but it will be noted here that Cohen's assumption that the conferment of power upon Wilt Chamberlain as a consequence of his economic wealth is a *negative* externality is open to question. The creation of multiple sources of power as a result of the market process, rather than power being held monopolistically by the state, may be regarded as a positive externality. Cohen appears to have no conception of how an unequal but diffuse distribution of resources and power may be socially beneficent, so that, for example, the concentration of capital in private financial institutions allows for large-scale speculative investment without the whole of society being exposed to the risk of failure. Indeed, it seems curious that Cohen is so distressed by the power that people may acquire as a side-effect of the possession of economic resources and yet simultaneously indifferent to the monopoly of political power held by the state, which he advocates being used against individuals whose actions threaten an egalitarian society: 'Any but the most utopian socialist must be willing under certain conditions to restrict the liberty of a few for the sake of the liberty of many' (Cohen 1995, p. 31). Cohen's critique of Nozick privileges centralized, monopolistic political power over decentralized, poly-centric economic power without offering any reason for treating one source or form of power as legitimate and the other as illegitimate (this point is made in a somewhat different way by Mack 2002).

As Nozick correctly stated, a just society must be one in which individuals have the freedom to use their justly acquired resources as they wish, even if the result is the creation of economic inequalities and the conferment of economic power upon those with more wealth than others. The alternative underlying Cohen's critique is close to tyrannical: a society in which third parties have the power to block voluntary exchanges of even the simplest goods and services and no person may save more resources than others or pass on a gift to their children that may be deemed to hinder the life chances of other children who did receive a similar gift.

Nozick's entitlement theory of justice provides one of the most incisive critiques of patterned theories of distribution and most compelling accounts of the justice of the distribution of income and wealth that arises spontaneously as a result of voluntary exchanges in the marketplace. A full appreciation of the ethics of the distribution of resources by the market must also take into account the empirical evidence of the role of economic value in the market process and the benefits that accrue to all members of society (including the poorest) when resources are distributed by the market.

Value, desert and the market process

The moral claim that people have to the rewards that result from market transactions may be further strengthened by the fact that, as discussed at length in Chapter 2, success in the marketplace is dependent upon our ability to meet the needs and satisfy the preferences of other people. Bill Gates and Mick Jagger, for example, have acquired their personal fortunes by providing goods and services (computer software, records and rock concerts) that people wish to purchase, whereas software developers or musicians who have not similarly satisfied popular demand will have failed to reap similar rewards. The attribution of desert to such outcomes, however, is highly problematic.

Miller (1989, 2001) has consistently argued that under conditions of perfect competition, market prices provide a non-arbitrary way of establishing the relative economic value of a good or service and therefore profits generated in an ideal marketplace provide a means of measuring and rewarding the economic contributions made by different individuals. In Miller's ideal market socialist society, price signals would therefore be used as the basis for the distribution of income and wealth according to desert:

> [I]f we want desert to form the basis of social practice – rather than being an idea that is used merely to form a series of idiosyncratic judgments – we need a non-arbitrary public standard to measure it. In this light, the attraction of market-based criterion is very considerable. If, therefore, we want to keep something like our present conception of desert and the practices that go with it, there is much to be said for using overt demand as a way of measuring the value of output. (Miller 1989, pp. 161–2)

Whereas Miller would not accept that in a capitalist society market mechanisms distribute income and wealth according to desert, it is contended that the informational properties of price signals could be harnessed by a market socialist society to direct output to where demand is greatest and reward those who put their abilities at the service of their fellows by meeting that demand.

The objection that individual conceptions of desert or merit may be incommensurable would appear to be neutralized by the fact that (as noted in the previous chapter) the basis of the price system is that it enables the reconciliation of seemingly incommensurable individual values; subjective individual preferences are translated into objective data available to any external observer so that it becomes possible to compare the value (price) of baked beans and mushrooms, or leather sofas and antique desks (Buchanan 1999). According to Miller (1989, p. 164), then, 'the market itself resolves the problem of aggregating values for discrete individuals into a general measure of value', so that it provides a convenient and apposite standard of desert.

Miller is correct that in the absence of distortions (for example, from protectionist policies), market prices and profits do reflect the subjective preferences of consumers and producers with regard to the value of different goods and services more effectively than any other means and that therefore price signals reflect the economic contribution of the people who provide those different goods and services. But it does not necessarily follow that the people who receive the greatest economic rewards from the market process deserve their returns.

At the most fundamental level it can be argued that luck plays a more important role in determining the rewards that people receive from their participation in the marketplace than desert. Sadurski (1985) has argued that the principal failing of the market in terms of social justice is that it rewards the scarcity of particular talents and attributes rather than desert. Because an individual happens to be highly intelligent or very physically able, and hence is able to make a particularly valuable contribution to society, this does not mean that they deserve the rewards that follow any more than a relatively less able person deserves less because through no fault of their own they cannot make a similar contribution. By rewarding those who have been lucky enough to be born with scarce abilities, it is argued that the market condemns those who have been less fortunate in the genetic lottery to a life of relative impoverishment. For Sadurski (1985, p. 116), distribution according to desert would not mean rewarding outcomes, for example in terms of productivity or meeting consumer demand, but rewarding the actual burdens that different individuals have assumed, in terms of 'some effort, sacrifice, work, risk, responsibility, inconvenience and so forth'.

It would seem hard to disagree with Sadurski that the rewards generated by the market are ultimately not deserved because people do not deserve the natural endowments that produce those rewards (this point was also forcefully made by Rawls 1999, p. 274).

However, Sadurski fails to provide a workable alternative measure of desert because it is not clear how incommensurable individual judgements of people's efforts, sacrifices, work, risks, responsibilities, inconvenience, and so on, can be reconciled in the absence of the price mechanism.

The attribution of desert to the distribution of rewards by the market is problematic because desert is an arbitrary, conscious judgment, whereas the value that the market process attaches to a person's contribution is the result of a non-arbitrary mechanism not subject to conscious control.

As Norman Barry (1979, pp. 137–8) has put it: 'The value of a person's services is determined by the impersonal forces of the market' so that 'earnings may merely reflect luck or ingenuity . . . rather than any semblance of moral merit'. Thus when the development of DVDs wiped out the market for video recorders it did not mean that video recorder manufacturers suddenly became any less deserving, but that as a result of the impersonal workings of the market the value of one product dramatically declined while another took its place among people's affections. Similarly, the producers of unsuccessful board games were no more deserving of failure than the inventors of the multi-million selling *Trivial Pursuit* deserved their fortunes.

In the marketplace, minimum effort can bring huge rewards and tremendous effort can bring scant returns: one hundred redundant miners may invest their life savings in a business and work all the hours of the day for many years only to see it fail, while a City investor may make a small fortune in a couple of hours by following a hunch on the performance of a particular stock. The market allocates rewards so arbitrarily that even if perfect competition were possible the outcomes produced could not be said to equate to desert or moral merit.

It is also the case that the motives of people who succeed in the marketplace may be entirely selfish, even if they do seek to realize their own ends by responding to the needs of other people of whom they have no personal knowledge. Indeed, the ethical case for the market as described in Chapter 2 rests upon the contention that the market is an institutional framework that leads both altruistic and selfish individuals to undertake socially beneficent actions. Attributing desert to market outcomes they be deemed problematic because it may seem to imply that a person motivated entirely by selfishness is more morally deserving than an altruist because they happen to have engaged in commercially successful practices.

While the market does reward the value of different economic contributions according to the subjective (and conceivably erroneous) judgments of other market participants, it is a mistake to attribute desert to such outcomes. Desert involves a conscious, arbitrary judgment that cannot be reconciled with an impersonal, non-arbitrary process that is beyond conscious control.

Yet the fact that the market leads people irrespective of their motives to respond to the needs of others of whom they have no personal knowledge is an important dimension of the moral case for the market. What becomes apparent, then, is that the positive moral quality belongs to the market process itself, rather than to market participants. The rewards that people receive in the marketplace, then, reflect the value that other people attach to their economic contributions, but they do not accord with any conception of desert or moral merit.

The difference principle and the benefits of inequality

It may be argued that the inequalities of income and wealth produced by the market are justified if they benefit the least advantaged or the least well-off more than their absence or minimization of such inequalities. This view forms the essence of John Rawls' 'difference principle' set out in his classic of egalitarian liberalism, *A Theory of Justice*: 'While the distribution of wealth and income need not be equal, it must be to everyone's advantage' (Rawls 1999, p. 53). Accordingly, an unequal distribution of income and wealth should be considered just if it is to everyone's advantage, including the least well-off. The 'difference principle' would appear to provide a particularly powerful argument against a strict egalitarianism that would logically prefer a relatively poor society in which every individual possessed equal wealth to an unequal society in which every individual enjoyed more resources than every member of the poorer society. Such strict egalitarianism, it can be argued, leads to the advocacy of 'equality of misery' over 'inequality of happiness' and hence to the creation of a 'levelled-down' society that is to the detriment of all, including the least advantaged and the least well-off.

It can be argued that the 'difference principle' fails to take into account the intrinsic value of equality and hence does not give proper weight to the full benefits of a strictly egalitarian society when compared to an unequal society. Temkin (2000, p. 155), for example, has asked, rhetorically and arguably somewhat bravely: 'do I really think there is some respect in which a world where only some are blind is worse than one where all are? Yes'. While Temkin does not go on to advocate blinding people in the name of egalitarianism, he does effectively make the point that some people (and conceivably those people may be the least advantaged and least well-off) may deem equality so inherently valuable that it trumps all other moral or material considerations. Indeed, it could be argued that being relatively poor in a wealthy society may be psychologically more harmful than being absolutely poor in an absolutely poor society.

Ultimately this must be a normative judgment, but it is relevant to note that very few egalitarians have been willing to argue that every person should receive the same income and wealth irrespective of who they are or what they do. Iris Marion Young (1990, p. 216), for example, has conceded that differential pay is likely to be necessary to reward hard work and extra effort, to compensate for the sacrifices involved in acquiring specialized skills, to provide incentives for undertaking undesirable work, and to reward above average productivity. The 'left-libertarian' philosopher Hillel Steiner (2002) has accepted that disparities of income and wealth may be justified if they result from 'disabling choices' by people who began from the same starting points in life. Even Marx's (1872, p. 20) famous mantra for the organization of the future socialist utopia was that every individual would receive material resources from the superabundant socialist storehouses 'according to his needs', rather than receive absolutely equal shares.

This section will argue that the benefits of economic prosperity and growth – which include practically all the benefits of well-being that we enjoy in an advanced civilization – outweigh the intrinsic value of an equal but impoverished society. And it will be contended that this is precisely the choice that we face between prosperous inequality and equal poverty.

Nozick's entitlement theory of justice provides a compelling account of the justice of economic transfers resulting from voluntary exchanges in the marketplace, but Nozick's depiction of a one-way transfer of wealth from basketball spectators to Wilt Chamberlain may give the impression that a market economy simply involves endless transfers of a fixed set of resources when in reality resources can be put to productive use to create more resources: how resources are allocated will determine what resources are available in the future. If resources are allocated efficiently to people who put them to productive use, then more resources can be produced for future distribution, whereas if resources are used inefficiently or left to spoil the inverse will be the case. Indeed, as noted earlier, Mack (2002, p. 81) has pointed out that Nozick's argument could have been made simpler and more effective if he had used the example of 'individuals increasing their holdings ... through unilateral action – through these individuals separately engaging in enhancing transformations of their assigned resources' rather than engaging in exchanges of seemingly fixed resources.

Inequalities of wealth between societies are principally attributable to how different societies have used the resources at their disposal in the past, not to their ability to somehow capture an unequal share of a fixed set of global assets. Hence, as Henderson (2004, p. 83) has described, 'rich countries are rich because their citizens produce more per head, not because they have secured privileged access to "the planet's goods", or to its "resources"'. Chapter 2 outlined why market economies generate levels of material prosperity that other economic systems cannot match, but in the context of the present discussion it is important to highlight the importance of inequalities of wealth and income to the process by which resources are used efficiently and economic growth takes place: differential rewards may motivate people to be as productive as possible; perform an epistemological function facilitating the efficient allocation of resources, and provide a means of funding investment and experimentation in new products and new ways of living. Moreover, progress cannot take place uniformly, but must always occur unequally, one echelon at a time, so that groups of people advance ahead of their contemporaries.

The material inequalities that arise from market exchange facilitate heuristic learning about the most economically successful courses of action and therefore about the needs and preferences of the many individuals dispersed throughout the economy. The fact that Wilt Chamberlain has become wealthy from playing basketball, for example, communicates information about the material rewards available from a successful career in the sport and hence how highly people value the opportunity to watch a great basketball player. Similarly, the fact that very few people become professional basketball players also communicates information about the likelihood of an individual becoming rich from such a career. In the same way, the fact that profits can be made from the provision of more prosaic goods and services communicates information about how highly people value those goods and services.

The informational signals provided by differential rewards in the marketplace are essential to the discovery of where there is greatest demand for people's skills and talents. As Sowell (1996, p. 75) has described, a dynamic, progressive economy requires the communication of such information via the unequal rewards received by different economic actors:

> When the automobile began to replace the horse and buggy, a conscientious, hard-working and intelligent buggy-manufacturer could not earn what someone with the same characteristics was earning in the automobile industry. That is precisely why and how people and capital were transferred out of the horse and buggy industry. It is why and how they (or others) were transferred into the automobile industry.

The movement of resources from the production of buggies into the production of cars was driven by the fact that greater rewards could be attained from the production of the latter; had such differential rewards not been available, such a spontaneous transfer of resources could not have occurred.

In the absence of price signals driven by unequal rewards an egalitarian society would either be subject to the under-supply of some goods and services, and the over-supply of others, or it would be necessary to force people to enter occupations where it was perceived that a shortage of labour existed (such a chaotic situation clearly existed within the 'shortage economy' of the former Soviet Union, see Boettke 2001, particularly Chapter 1). Differential rewards, then, perform a motivational and epistemological function: they inform market participants where they can maximize their economic contribution and provide pecuniary motivation for so doing.

Cohen (1995, 2000) has objected that a society cannot be considered just if its members require material incentives in order to maximize their productivity. For Cohen, a just society is one where people are motivated by a sense of duty or commitment to others rather than the lure of personal gain. Cohen's argument, however, fails to take into account the fact that even if an entire population was altruistically motivated to maximize productivity out of a commitment to creating a socialist utopia, for example, in the absence of the epistemological function performed by differential rewards they would have no way of knowing where or how they should expend their efforts in order to maximize productivity. While, as noted in Chapter 2, motivation is required if people are to take advantage of the information communicated by prices and profit oppurtunities in the marketplace, motivation without information is futile.

It has been argued that in the real world, individuals are not in a position to change occupations as effortlessly as may be implied by such a description of the market process. According to Dworkin (2000, p. 100), discovering what one can earn in different occupations requires trying each occupation and 'in the case of some professions, trying is impossible without half a lifetime of preparation'. This is, of course, a truism: we do not know exactly how much we might earn as a barrister or as a chef, for example, without the opportunity to try our hand at these occupations.

While price signals are not perfect communicators of information, they do nevertheless provide the best possible indication of the likely rewards of different occupations. Price signals tell us that an averagely successful barrister is likely to earn more than an averagely successful chef, though a highly successful chef working in a top restaurant will probably earn more than a relatively unsuccessful barrister. The information communicated by the price mechanism facilitates comparative judgments, although individual abilities will of course influence the precise rewards different individuals will receive from different careers. Moreover, some individuals will be able to garner previously unrealized rewards from their occupations by entrepreneurially discovering new opportunities, new niches and new ways of working.

Unequal rewards ensure that labour and capital are directed to where they are most needed. This can be achieved only where no attempt is made to make the rewards for different occupations correspond with people's beliefs about the moral merit of those occupations; any attempt to do so would imply the possession of objective knowledge about the social worth of different occupations, knowledge that simply does not exist. Differential rewards can only perform their function as incentives and communicators of information if they reflect the subjective choices of consumers and producers in the marketplace, rather than individual opinions about moral merit. The contention – usually but not exclusively made by market socialists – that the allocative and distributive functions of the price mechanism can be separated, and the allocative function used but the distributive function abandoned (for example, Carens 1981; Rawls 1999, p. 241), neglects this crucial function of differential rewards in directing labour and capital to where demand is greatest. Should incomes be determined by a deliberative process, rather than by the impersonal workings of the market, then unless by pure chance a deliberately chosen salary was equal to that that would have been allocated by the market (in which case the deliberative process has served no purpose), a misallocation of capital would take place, meaning that resources would not be allocated to where they were most needed and economic inefficiency would result.

Inequalities also contribute to economic growth and social progress by facilitating investment in new products and experiments with different lifestyles without the whole of society being required to fund such experimentation or give majority approval to new innovations. As Adam Smith (1982a, pp. 179–85) noted in the eighteenth century, the pursuit of luxury and convenience by the rich raised living standards throughout society because the rich paid for new products and research that ultimately benefited all. In order to enjoy the luxury of fast transportation, for example, the rich paid for new roads to be laid, invested in the development of new carriages and in the breeding of faster horses, all of which benefited other people. Similarly, to give two contemporary examples, people who first purchased personal computers and mobile phones when those products were beyond the means of most individuals paid for the technological research and development that has led to these products being available at a price that essentially all members of the same societies can now afford. While these societies are ostensibly not equal in terms of incomes, over time few 'luxuries' will not become available to all:

> If today in the United States or western Europe the relatively poor can have a car or a refrigerator, an airplane trip or a radio, at the cost of reasonable part of their income, this was made possible because in the past others with larger incomes were able to spend on what was then a luxury... What today may seem extravagance or even waste, because it is enjoyed by the few and even undreamed of by the masses, is payment for the experimentation with a style of living that will eventually become available to many. (Hayek 1960, p. 44)

Although the well-off intend only the enjoyment of the luxuries that they alone can afford, their actions in fact serve an important social function, funding research and experimentation, testing new products and new ways of living, which, if popular, will in time become accessible to all. Without wealthy individuals to perform this function, an egalitarian society would have to set aside a particular category of people to test new products and lifestyles to see if they should be made available to the whole population.

This does mean that at any one point in time there will be people who do not have access to 'the best' that society can offer, so that some people will be able to enjoy exotic foreign holidays while others cannot, or where there is a market in healthcare some people will have access to innovative treatments that others do not. This is unavoidable unless particular choices (whether exotic holidays or new healthcare treatments) are to be prohibited until and unless they can be made available universally (which is practically impossible unless provision is made free at the point of supply). But those people who do not have access to 'the best' will still enjoy a lifestyle that a generation earlier would have been the preserve of only the most privileged and, in turn, their children will no doubt enjoy a lifestyle that was beyond their parents' means. It is unfortunate that progress cannot occur simultaneously and that attempts to make progress uniform can only destroy the process that brings advance, but rather like a team of mountaineers scaling a cliff face, those following the advance party will be able to follow the route laid by the pioneers to ascend more quickly than would otherwise have been possible (Acton 1993, pp. 232–3; Hayek 1960, pp. 42–5).

Inequality is essential to an efficient and dynamic economy that is able to develop and to create wealth. Differential rewards act as an incentive to motivate people to maximize their contribution to society and communicate the information necessary to ensure that their efforts are expended in a socially beneficent manner. Inequalities of wealth and income also facilitate investment in new products and experiments in living as the rich seek to create a more luxurious or comfortable life for themselves and by so doing fund research and development that will eventually make such a lifestyle accessible to even the poorest members of society. Moreover, economic and social progress itself implies unequal steps forward, as different people push back the boundaries in different areas. The inequalities that result from market exchanges must be said to be in the interests of all, including the least advantaged and least well-off, because prosperity and economic growth could not be achieved without economic inequality.

Inequality, economic mobility and equality of opportunity

Economic inequalities are both essential to and an inevitable feature of the economic growth that benefits all members of society. It is not the case, however, that the relatively well-off are able to capture an inordinate share of the benefits that result from economic prosperity. It is true that some wealthy people do successfully re-invest their wealth to create more wealth and that in the context of the model of static equilibrium used within neo-classical economics – in which wealth creation is understood as a process of transforming given resources into goods and services using known methods of production or trade – the wealthy do appear to possess an in-built advantage that guarantees their future success. But empirical evidence does not support the portrayal of a market economy as one in which the poor are doomed to economic failure and the rich are guaranteed continued success.

In fact, the evidence suggests that within real world market economies there has been no polarization between rich and poor during the past century: the rich do not get richer while the poor get poorer. On the contrary, there is evidence of high levels of economic mobility within the unequal income distribution of capitalist societies (Choi 1999, pp. 244–5). In the United States, for example, a society often criticized for its alleged entrenched inequalities (for example Callinicos 2000), of those people who were among the poorest 20 per cent of the population in 1979, within ten years more had climbed into the richest 20 per cent than remained in the poorest quintile. Indeed, 86 per cent of the poorest 20 per cent in 1979 had improved their position within ten years, not only in absolute terms, but also relative to other people, as had 60 per cent of the second poorest quintile. In all but the richest 20 per cent, people were more likely to move up or down the income scale than to remain in the same position, and in every category (again, bar the richest 20 per cent for obvious reasons) there was more upward than downward mobility (Choi 1999, p. 246).

Indeed, empirical analysis of economic freedom (defined *inter alia* in terms of levels of taxation and government regulation) and income distribution in over one hundred countries between 1975 and 1995 provided evidence that the economic growth engendered by economic freedom led the incomes of the poor to rise at a faster rate than those of the rich to the extent that it could be argued that increased economic freedom was positively related to economic equality (Berggren 1999).

Despite the in-built advantage that the wealthy would appear to possess, the poor are able to improve their position relative to the rich in a market economy because those who have been economically successful in the past may be at a disadvantage when it comes to future economic success. Contrary to the neo-classical model of wealth generation simply involving the transformation of given resources using known methods, the key to economic success is in fact entrepreneurship: the discovery of new profit opportunities, new prices and new ways of doing things holds the key to profit maximization (Kirzner 1973 provides the classic account). According to Choi (1999, p. 254), success does not necessarily breed success: 'if we have met success in the past with certain ways of doing business and become rich, we are less likely to deviate from them', whereas, 'we are more likely to explore different possibilities, if we have not had much success with our approach'. The key to successful entrepreneurial activity is not to run fastest along the known path – where the rich will indeed have a head start over their competitors – but to discover a different route or even a new destination.

Hence, an individual who has yet to experience success in the employment market may be more inclined to pursue educational opportunities, re-train or seek entry to a new industry, compared to an individual who has been successful in the past and may therefore be more inclined to attempt to repeat a previously successful formula. By joining an emergent industry or acquiring cutting-edge skills, an individual starting from a relatively lowly position may be able to reap substantial rewards. Similarly, a firm that has been successful in the past may be reluctant to implement new management techniques or introduce new products, whereas a firm without the same history may be particularly eager to seek out and implement new approaches. It is for this reason that numerous large and previously successful electrical companies, including IBM, turned down opportunities to invest in computer technology prior to the personal computing boom, thereby allowing a host of new entrants to dominate the marketplace, just as half a century earlier previously successful companies declined opportunities to invest in telephone and radio technology, also leaving the field open for new entrants to prosper (Choi 1999).

The fact that inequality within a market economy is dynamic does not, of course, mean that the market provides equality of opportunity. On the contrary, equality of opportunity cannot exist where individuals are free to dispose of their own property as they wish because people are always liable to use this freedom to provide their children with benefits and opportunities that (by definition) other children will not enjoy. Moreover, at an even more fundamental level, the natural distribution of talents and abilities means that some individuals will inevitably begin life with advantages that others do not share.

It should also be noted that the idea of equality of opportunity appears to imply that life is a race from a single start line to a single finish line in which (without some form of intervention) some people are better equipped than others and hence destined to win. This conception is erroneous because, simply: 'life is not a race in which we all compete for a prize which someone has established' (Nozick 1974, p. 235). In reality there is no single race to a single finish line in pursuit of one prize, but a myriad of different people simultaneously striving for a myriad of different things. It is for this reason that Nozick (1974, pp. 235–9) rejected the contention that procedural justice requires that all individuals have equal starting points in life: equal starting points are not relevant because life is not a single race from a single starting point to a single finish line, but multiple events all starting at different times from different starting points to different finish lines.

Because life is not a single race between two fixed points, attempts to achieve equality of opportunity also encounter profound epistemological obstacles (in addition to the injustice of prohibiting inter-generational bequests). The notion that the education system might be used to culturally compensate people whose families have not imbued them with the most useful norms and values (considered, for example, by Rawls 1999, p. 63) raises the question of how such culturally useful values are to be identified and then taught. The values that are particularly useful to a plumber, for example, are likely to be different to those that are especially useful to a teacher or an accountant. The idea that the education system can fully compensate for the failure of particular families to teach important cultural values is based upon the assumption that policy-makers can identify the socially useful values and devise means to transmit them – no mean feat given the failure of state education in so many advanced countries to teach even fairly basic skills to many students.

Similarly, a transfer of resources that only takes into account financial capital, and neglects human, cultural and social capital, may unwittingly heighten rather than reduce inequalities of opportunity by further disadvantaging those individuals who have high levels of financial capital but lack the human, cultural and social capital necessary to make productive use of their economic assets.

In common with any economy in which the institution of the family exists, a market economy cannot provide equality of opportunity. But it is nevertheless the case that market economies offer more opportunities for social and economic mobility than any other economic system and that this mobility is principally based upon an individual's ability to satisfy the subjective needs of other people, rather than upon the arbitrary judgement of a political official (in the case of a planned economy) or the fact that a person happened to be born into a particular caste or family (in the case of a feudal society).

Poverty, sufficiency and a guaranteed minimum income

It is frequently contended that widespread poverty still exists amidst the prosperity of contemporary market economies and that such poverty is increasing. Callinicos (2000, p. 9), for example, has claimed that the proportion of the UK population living in poverty increased between 1979 and 1995, because more people received a net household income below the national median household income at the later date. Similarly, research published by the Joseph Rowntree Foundation claimed that child poverty in the UK had increased between 1979 and 1999 because more children lived in households with income below half of the national median at the later date (Howarth *et al.* 1999). A similar picture was portrayed in a 2004 report of the House of Commons Select Committee on Work and Pensions which stated that 'The number of children in poverty has increased threefold in the last 25 years', on the basis that the number of children living in households with income less than 60 per cent of the national median has trebled during the last quarter century (House of Commons Work and Pensions Committee 2004, p. 17).

These studies, however, do not really concern poverty but equality. According to their logic if the real income of every member of society quadrupled, this increased prosperity would lead to an increase in the number of people living in poverty as the gap between rich and poor would also quadruple: if one person earned £10,000 per year and another £100,000, the gap between their annual incomes would be £90,000; if the income of both quadrupled, the poor person would earn £40,000 a year, the rich individual £400,000, and the gap would become £360,000. Hence, an increase in wealth spread evenly throughout society will increase inequality and, according to some, increase poverty, even though every one has become wealthier. According to these measures poverty would still exist in a society where the whole population owned a personal yacht, but the richest people owned six yachts each and the poorest only one. The 'poverty' that these studies measure, then, can only be eradicated by the creation of an egalitarian society.

In reality, actual material deprivation (that is, absolute poverty) is zero (or very close to zero) in contemporary market economies. The prosperity that market economies have generated in the past century means that no one need now go without food, shelter and clothing; it is now practically unheard of for a child to grow up in a house without a television and a telephone, let alone electricity or running water (National Statistics Office 2004).

Nevertheless, it is at least theoretically possible that if market forces alone were allowed to determine the distribution of resources without some form of 'safety net' a small proportion of the population could face periods without an income and thereby experience genuine hardship. The vagaries of the operation of labour markets, for example, are likely to mean that some people will experience periods without work and it is conceivable that some may be unemployed for long periods. Equally, natural disasters may leave people without the means of their subsistence: a farmer may find their estate and assets destroyed by a hurricane, and their insurance company gone bankrupt, or a flood may wipe out a small business that was inadequately insured.

Amartya Sen (1985) has argued that within the context of Nozick's entitlement theory an individual (or group of individuals) could face destitution, starvation and even death without there being any diminution of society's overall wealth and without any injustice occurring; a person may lose their job and their income, become destitute and ultimately starve to death without having any claim on the resources of other people, all completely 'legitimately' within Nozick's schema. For Sen, the morality of a social order that could justify such a situation must be questioned.

Certainly, the question of 'the starving man in the liberal polity' (Conway 1995, p. 20) is an important test of the ethics of the market: does an individual who (for whatever reason) does not possess the means of their subsistence have a legal or a moral claim to the resources of others within the context of a free market economy? Conway (1995, pp. 20–4) has argued that a liberal polity may be justified in forcing parents to provide for their children (though exactly how this is to be done is not specified), but that adults who become destitute (for whatever reason) have no claim on the resources of others: they may appeal to the charity of their fellows, but the principles of entitlement and self-ownership of the products of one's own labour mean that the destitute cannot forcibly take other people's justly held resources in order to survive. Thus, for Conway, any form of statutory welfare provision is untenable. While such a position is intellectually consistent, it nevertheless raises practical and ethical difficulties.

First, it means, precisely as Sen (1985) objected, that (theoretically at least) an individual could starve to death in such an 'ideal' without their rights being infringed, without any wrong being committed and without any person or body being responsible. It is hard not to view such a position as being morally callous towards the unfortunate or plain foolish.

Second, it would appear to negate the idea that the state has a meaningful role in a market society. If we accept the legitimacy of the state as the ultimate legal authority, the protector of private property rights and the body responsible for, for example, national defence, then it would appear reasonable that the state should also have a role as the insurer of last resort: the provision of a minimum level of social assistance and insurance would seem to be a reasonable function of a minimal state.

Third it might be objected that if people genuinely cared for the destitute they would voluntarily give their resources to them but this neglects the collective action and free-rider problems that arise here – that is, who is 'responsible' and therefore should pay for those in need.

For these reasons it is argued here that it is an appropriate role of the state to provide 'the certainty of a given minimum of sustenance for all' as part of the framework within which the market operates (Hayek 1944, p. 89). It is important, however, to emphasize the distinction between guaranteeing subsistence, guaranteeing a certain standard of living (for example, ensuring that the incomes of train drivers or accountants do not fall below a specified level) and (re)distributing income and wealth according to a preferred pattern of distribution. Only the first of these three alternatives is compatible with a free society and a market economy.

It has been argued that to advocate the provision of a guaranteed minimum income by the state logically implies an acceptance that the distribution of income and wealth cannot be left solely to the market and that this therefore opens up the whole question of distributional justice in the marketplace. According to Gamble (1996, p. 49): 'once that concession has been made, the argument about social justice re-emerges'; the 'concession' that some basic income level should be determined and provided by political authority is said to re-introduce the role of political authority in determining all income and wealth distribution.

Gamble's objection, however, fails to appreciate the above outlined distinction between ensuring that no one falls below a basic minimum standard on the one hand and guaranteeing a certain category of people a given quality of life or imposing a particular pattern of distribution upon a society on the other. The second and third alternatives would compromise the role of the market as the mechanism by which resources are distributed throughout society, whereas the first alternative concerns the role of the state in providing a framework within which the market operates. Of course, as noted in Chapter 2, even a minimal state has to be funded, presumably from taxation and conceivably from compulsory general taxation. Hence the provision of a guaranteed level of subsistence (in common with the other functions of a minimal state) will involve a compromise between the conviction that no one may confiscate another person's justly held resources and the belief that in the context of the prosperity that market economies have created no one should be denied sufficient resources on which to live, whatever the cause of their predicament.

It is important to note, however, that few (if any) citizens of free market economies would have recourse to such a guarantee. Most of the situations in which individuals would require support from a state-supplied basic minimum income are extreme situations where an individual was left without any means of providing their own subsistence that few people would encounter in their lifetimes. For most people private insurance would provide the financial safety net in the event of unemployment, accident or other personal trauma, most frequently at a level far greater than the state provided basic minimum.

The advocacy of a guaranteed minimum income raises a number of important secondary issues. First, it is possible that productive members of a polity may be exploited by the 'voluntary destitution' of individuals who choose to live on the minimum income and not work in preference to working for a relatively low wage. It is imperative that the minimum income is set at a rate at which it does not create a perverse incentive against obtaining paid employment and creates a positive incentive for purchasing private insurance against risks such as unemployment or ill-health. To attach obligations to the minimum income, such as undertaking some form of community service in return for payment, would however be inconsistent with the principle of a guaranteed minimum. For this reason it has to be accepted that where a minimum income was guaranteed it would be possible for some people to free-ride on the contributions on others

(Brittan 1995, p. 243 has argued that this may be a positive benefit of a guaranteed minimum income).

Second, what constitutes a basic minimum standard is not fixed, but is open to subjective interpretation: what Western Europeans and North Americans would consider a basic minimum may be deemed a life of luxury in parts of the developing world. While the basic standard should be set as close to subsistence level as possible, it is clear that there will be an element of subjectivity as to the level at which any given polity sets its basic minimum.

Third, while a guaranteed minimum income may be achievable only where a functioning market economy has first created an appropriate level of material prosperity, the morality of denying such a standard to people who happen not to live within a particular polity may be questioned. Increased globalization – in terms of increased global migration, the reduced salience of national political boundaries and our superior knowledge of the lives of other people living in distant countries – has important implications for questions of social welfare. Miller (2001) has noted that it will probably become untenable to support generous welfare states in the developed world and simultaneously deny those same benefits to people living in the poorest parts of the world. There is undoubtedly a strong moral case for extending a guaranteed minimum income to the developing world, though the economic or practical feasibility of such a proposal is highly questionable. It is therefore proposed here that the basic minimum income should be applied within the geo-political boundaries of single nation-states.

While a market economy will generate a level of prosperity that will effectively banish poverty, it is argued that this wealth also enables the citizens of free market economies to be guaranteed a subsistence level income to ensure that no one need ever go without the basic essentials of life as a result of a loss of income due to some misfortune or foolishness. This is not a redistributive measure, but should constitute part of the basic institutional framework within which a market economy operates.

Conclusion

A market economy is a wealth-generating mechanism that has created unprecedented levels of material prosperity in those societies where market institutions have been established. This chapter has shown that while the market produces inequalities of income and wealth that bear no relation to need or desert, and are not combined with equality of opportunity, market participants are nevertheless entitled to the differential rewards that follow from voluntary exchanges in the marketplace. Indeed, the requirements of procedural justice can only be satisfied by an economy in which individuals are allowed to dispose of their resources as they see fit, irrespective of whether as a result some individuals accumulate more wealth than others.

Moreover, economic inequality is an essential ingredient of wealth generation. An increase in prosperity, and social progress more generally, can only take place in echelon fashion, with some people advancing ahead of others. Economic growth cannot occur simultaneously and uniformly across a whole society.

Furthermore, the possibility of garnering an unequal reward provides an incentive to purposeful action and communicates information about the most socially beneficent use of resources.

The inequalities that do exist within market economies, however, are dynamic rather than static: it is not the case that the rich get richer while the poor get poorer. On the contrary, the nature of entrepreneurship means that those who have yet to be economically successful may be at a distinct advantage when it comes to the innovation crucial to future commercial success.

The prosperity of contemporary market economies has made it possible and legitimate to guarantee every individual a minimum income. The state should provide a minimum level of subsistence, rather than a particular income that a group or person is thought to deserve. The guiding principle of such a proposal is that no one should be allowed to fall below a certain level, while, equally, there should be no limit as to how high a person can rise. A market economy combined with a guaranteed minimum income will be one in which a high level of prosperity can be enjoyed in the knowledge that no person will be without sufficient income for their subsistence.

This chapter has shown that only the distribution of income and wealth produced by a market economy can be considered just. While the market produces inequalities that bear no relation to need or desert, and are not combined with equality of opportunity, it is nevertheless the case that – in terms of distribution – a market economy is a moral economy. This book will now consider the second aspect of 'social justice' essential to an ethical assessment of the market: the alleged exploitative nature of many of the apparently voluntary transactions that people enter into in the marketplace.

5
Exploitation and Coercion

This chapter will examine the second aspect of 'social justice' that must be taken into account in an ethical assessment of the market: the claim that many of the supposedly voluntary exchanges that take place in a market economy are in fact founded upon exploitation and coercion.

The contention that a market economy is characterized by the exploitation of the poor by the rich, of labour by capital and of the powerless by the powerful, and that in a market economy many people's choices are so limited that they are effectively coerced into undertaking undesirable, soul-destroying or hazardous work, forms one of the most important and enduring ethical critiques of the market. According to Wood (1995, p. 157), a capitalist market economy is inherently exploitative:

> [S]ince under capitalism there are vast differences in economic power and ample opportunity in the market system for the strong to use these differences to their advantage, capitalism is...a highly exploitative social order, perhaps the most exploitative the world has ever known.

McIntosh (1972, pp. 245–5) has claimed that the seemingly mutually advantageous contracts that people enter into in a market economy mask the coercive nature of economic power in the market:

> [T]ake a contract between a landlord and a sharecropper. From one point of view, both benefit from the relationship, which is

hence ... noncoercive. From another point of view, however, the landlord may be in such an advantageous bargaining position that he can impose highly unfair and exploitative terms. From this point of view the relationship is injurious to the sharecropper ... Economic influence is best regarded as a form of coercion.

It is argued that the claims to self-ownership and individual freedom that classical liberals and libertarians put at the heart of their moral case for the market economy are hollow because in reality a market economy enables those with more resources than others to use that economic power to exploit and coerce those who have less.

'Exploitation' and 'coercion' are notoriously slippery concepts that can give rise to a multiplicity of meanings and interpretations (Aarstol 1991; Howarth 1990, 1992; Nozick 1997; Wertheimer 1996), but in the context of the present discussion it is possible to arrive at definitions of each that satisfactorily express the sense in which they are used when referring to power and choice within a market economy. Following Wilkinson (2004) and Wertheimer (1996), exploitation may be defined as 'taking unfair advantage', for example as has been claimed occurs when workers are paid less than the true value of what they produce or are paid less than the salary that a 'perfectly competitive' market would allocate. Coercion may be defined as 'forcing a person to do something they would not otherwise do', such as when a mugger forces a person to handover their money or face serious injury (an example of a 'coercive offer') or when a slave owner forces their slaves to live and work under their control.

The claim that the market is inherently exploitative and/or coercive does not rest upon isolated incidents where individuals may have been judged to have taken unfair advantage or forced people to do something they would not otherwise have done, but concerns 'the coerciveness or otherwise of institutions and mechanisms; capitalism in its regular workings and not just the isolated event' (Howarth 1992, p. 80). The discussion that follows therefore does not concern isolated examples, but the nature of the market as an institution. To this end, this chapter will examine three distinct dimensions of the ethical critique of a market economy as an exploitative and coercive economic system and in response show why this ethical critique should be rejected.

Plan of the chapter

First, this chapter will set out the claim that many of the practices fundamental to a market economy – in particular using other people as a means to achieve one's own ends, profiting from other people's needs and wants, and engaging in arbitrage – are inherently exploitative. This often intuitive belief that the market is inherently exploitative underlies the more systematic accounts of market exploitation and coercion that will then be considered, beginning with classical and contemporary Marxist critiques of capitalism and then presenting other accounts that relate to the inequalities of bargaining power that exist in the marketplace.

In response to these arguments it will first be shown that activities such as using other people as a means of achieving one's own ends, profiting from other people's needs and arbitrage, are in fact necessary features of any advanced economy and, moreover, have positive moral qualities. The chapter will then turn to the more systematic and substantive critiques, where it will be shown that the common depiction of negotiations between monopsonistic employers and individual employees bears little relation to labour market negotiations in real world market economies. It will then be noted that individual choices are inevitably limited wherever people make legitimate choices that impact on others. The fact that an individual may have to make choices that they would ideally not wish to make does not mean that they have been exploited or coerced. Finally, this chapter will answer the contemporary Marxist critiques of capitalist exploitation. Here, it will be shown that the Marxist view of entrepreneurial profit neglects the crucial role that the owners of private companies perform in the management and organization of the economy that would have to be replicated in a non-market economy.

The exploitative, coercive marketplace

The claim that the market is fundamentally exploitative undoubtedly has an intuitive rhetorical power because participation in a market economy very often does involve using other people as a means to achieve one's own ends, profiting from other people's needs and engaging in arbitrage. As Ratnapala (2003, p. 213) has described, 'the notion of profiting from dealings with others seems intuitively wrong to many people, even when profits are gained by perfectly legal transactions'. Suspicion of profiteering and arbitrage has a long history, dating from the Ancient Greeks onwards (Muller 2002; Ratnapala 2003), and this suspicion underlies the more systematic accounts of exploitation developed in the nineteenth and twentieth centuries.

Adam Smith's (1981, pp. 26–7) famous butcher, brewer and baker quote, discussed in the second chapter, describes three tradespeople who provide for others not out of altruistic benevolence, but out of 'regard to their own interest'; they produce and sell meat, beer and bread at a profit in order to provide the means of their own subsistence. Given that the butcher, brewer and baker use their customers as a means of achieving their own ends, it could be claimed that they are engaged in inherently exploitative behaviour.

Similarly, it may be argued that to derive personal benefit from the satisfaction of another person's needs and, in particular, from their vulnerabilities, constitutes exploitation. Matthews (1998), for example, has argued that it is 'morally inappropriate' for people to profit from the health needs of others that have arisen as a result of epidemiological misfortune.

It might similarly be argued, to provide another example, that it is morally wrong for a home security company to target elderly people living alone who may feel (and be) particularly vulnerable to crime in order to sell burglar alarms; to profit from such actions might be judged exploitative. This argument may be further developed to suggest that unscrupulous producers may actively create demand for their goods and services by exploiting people's insecurities and vulnerabilities. A clinic offering cosmetic surgery, for example, may create a demand for its services via advertising that fuels people's insecurities about their physical appearance.

The market has also been alleged to be inherently exploitative because of the importance of arbitrage (buying low and selling high) to its operation. There is a long-standing and widely held popular belief that every object has one true value and therefore to sell a good for a higher price than what was originally paid for it, or for a higher price than it cost to produce, is to engage in underhand and ultimately exploitative activity (Child 1998; Ratnapala 2003).

This chapter will now present the more systematic critiques of the market as exploitative and coercive, beginning with the critiques drawn from the Marxist tradition of political and economic thought.

Marxist theories of power and exploitation

The Marxist tradition of social, political and economic thought offers probably the most systematic treatment of the concept of exploitation in the academic literature. This should be no surprise given that exploitation was at the heart of Marx's theory of the workings of capitalism.

According to Marx, all social orders where a surplus of goods was produced other than communism were characterized by exploitative social relations. But it was under capitalism that exploitation was particularly acute and visible, as the class that owned the means of production ruthlessly exploited the workers they employed. According to Marx (1976, p. 342), the bourgeoisie were 'vampire-like', a class that sustained itself by sucking the very life-blood from the proletariat.

The classical Marxist view of exploitation was founded upon the labour theory of value that decreed that the value of any good was the sum of the labour that had gone into its transformation from raw material to exchangeable commodity. It was claimed that in a market economy, the capitalists derived profits by paying their workers less than the value of the labour they contributed to the production process and pocketing the shortfall, otherwise known as the 'surplus value'. The workers had no choice but to sell their labour on the terms demanded by the capitalist because they had no other means of subsistence. Hence, in a market economy those who did not own the means of production could only survive by selling their labour to the capitalists who did own the means of production, who must in turn exploit labour in order to generate their profits (Bose 1980; Carver 1987; Marx 1950, 1976).

This view of exploitation as the extraction of surplus value encounters the serious problem that the labour theory of value upon which it is based is demonstrably false. Put simply, the value of any good or service is not determined by the amount of labour time required to produce it. It is clear that rare goods (such as fine wines or antique coins) have a value that bears no relation to the labour that went into their production, that the labour of different individuals does not produce the same results (a highly skilled craftsperson can produce in a day what may take another person a week), that some goods require a large amount of labour time to produce but do not have a correspondingly high value (an academic book may take years to write but have little commercial value) and that identical goods produced using identical labour time may have different values in different places and at different times according to the fluctuations of supply and demand.

While a small number of Marxists still hold to the validity of the labour theory of value, rather like the people who still maintain that the sun orbits the earth despite the irrefutable evidence to the contrary, most contemporary Marxist scholars accept that the labour theory of value is erroneous. Today, the Marxist conception of capitalist exploitation is instead predicated on the much more straightforward claim that capitalist profit is based upon the expropriation of the product of the workers' labour, irrespective of whether it is that labour that creates or determines value:

> What raises the charge of exploitation is not that the capitalist gets some of the value the worker produces, but that he gets some of the value of *what* the worker produces. Whether or not the workers produce value, they produce the product, that which has value. (Cohen 1979, p. 354; see also Carver 1987; Cohen 1995; Roemer 1982; Schwartz 1995)

Exploitation, it is alleged, occurs when non-producing capitalists claim as their profits a portion (usually referred to as the 'surplus') of the product created by the productive class in the form of profits, rent or interest.

Marxist theories of exploitative require that a surplus is produced and that one group of individuals has a monopoly of the means of production that gives them control over the productive resources of society, including the men and women who must work to produce that which has value. Here, the Marxist conception of exploitation finds common ground with non-Marxist theories that have at their centre the asymmetries of bargaining power deemed inherent to a market economy.

Asymmetries of bargaining power and exploitation

Perhaps the most enduring and powerful critique of a market economy as inherently exploitative is the contention that the asymmetries of bargaining power that exist between those with many economic resources and those with relatively few enable the rich and powerful to exploit the relatively poor and vulnerable. While this view is undoubtedly central to Marxist views of capitalist exploitation (for example, Carver 1987; Cohen 1995), it is also important to non-Marxist critiques of classical liberalism and libertarianism. At the start of the twentieth century the New Liberal scholar L. T. Hobhouse (1994, pp. 39–40), for example, described bargaining between employers and employees in a free market in the following terms:

> Free contract did not solve the question of the helpless child. It left it to be 'exploited' by the employer in his own interest . . . If the child was helpless, was the grown-up person, man or woman, in a much better position? Here was the owner of a mill employing five hundred hands. Here was the operative possessed of no alternative means of subsistence seeking employment. Suppose them to bargain as to terms. If the bargain failed, the employer lost one man and had four hundred and ninety-nine to keep his mill going... During the same days the operative might have nothing to eat and might see his children going hungry. Where was the effective liberty in such an arrangement?

Because an employer was able to operate almost indefinitely without taking on an additional employee, while each worker would only be able to survive a relatively short time without paid employment, it was contended that when the two parties negotiated all the bargaining power rested with the employer who was able to strike an agreement on the most favourable terms. Just as a child was 'helpless' in the marketplace, liable to be exploited by unscrupulous capitalists, so it was claimed that in the absence of government intervention the majority of adult men and women were similarly powerless to agree an employment contract that did not constitute exploitation or coercion.

It is argued that in contemporary capitalist societies few (if any) people are employed in working conditions harmful to health or for subsistence-level wages because of government regulation and intervention, but the differential economic power of firms and their employees nevertheless enables companies to employ workers at a wage rate below that which would be set by a truly competitive, free market of the kind described in the neo-classical model of perfect competition:

The owner of capital is able to command a premium which reflects simply the social scarcity of the resource he brings to the transaction… Since [the employer] can command more, the employee must accept less than he would obtain under a competitive equilibrium. (Miller 1989, p. 194; see also Zimmerman 1981, p. 142)

According to Miller (1989, pp. 194–5), in a truly competitive equilibrium a person's income and wealth would be determined by the interplay of the natural facts of the world and the personal characteristics of the individual – such as the resources that are available, people's tastes and preferences and an individual's personal skills, talents and efforts. In a capitalist market economy, however, the resources held by the capitalists relative to their employees allow the capitalist to set a wage rate that bears little relation to the natural or personal facts that would determine economic rewards in a truly competitive market economy. Because an employee has to work in order to live a worthwhile life, 'The worker's needs and the employer's command of resources together create the power relationship that culminates in exploitation' (Miller 1989, p. 195).

The view that many people employed in a market economy are not paid the true value of their economic contribution or receive wages below what they would be paid in a perfectly competitive market has been translated into public policy as an important justification for the minimum wage legislation introduced by the governments of many liberal democracies, including the UK and the US (Wilkinson 2004). Similar arguments have also been applied to the relationships between firms from developed nations and their employees in the developing world; it is argued that the bargaining power advantage enjoyed by international corporations over the populations of Third World countries leads to exploitation in the form of subsistence wage employment often in atrocious working conditions (for example, McMurtry 1997).

Coercion and choice: 'your money or your life'

Asymmetries of bargaining power are claimed to lead to exploitation because economically powerless individuals are forced to enter into transactions that they would not otherwise accept. Hence, this category of capitalist exploitation also involves capitalist coercion, although it is possible that one may be coerced without necessarily being exploited, if a person is forced to do work that is not inherently exploitative or is well-remunerated (though the distinction may be in large part semantic).

In the classical Marxist view of exploitation, workers are forced into accepting employment under the conditions of wage-slavery determined by the capitalist because they have no plausible alternative: they face a 'choice' between working for the capitalist or starvation. A fundamentally identical view of the market as inherently coercive is advanced by many contemporary scholars. Olsaretti (1998, pp. 58–9), for example, offers the following account of the choice faced by a worker in a notional free market: 'P is a worker who chooses to sell his labour to employer Q. The choice which he faces is to either work for Q at a very low wage, or to be unemployed and eventually starve.'

While individuals in contemporary market economies are rarely claimed to face a choice between employment by capitalists or starvation, it is more commonly alleged that 'workers have a choice between taking a well-paid (but still relatively unsatisfying) job and going on welfare (which is usually somewhat worse)' (Zimmerman 1981, p. 121). It is contended, then, that within a market economy workers face a 'choice' between one undesirable alternative and another even more undesirable alternative because their choices have been so framed by the economically powerful. Hence, a market economy coerces people into accepting alternatives that they would not otherwise choose in a non-market economy.

Scholars who have depicted the market as coercive have employed the analogy of robbery by a highwayman – who gives the alternatives of 'your money or your life' – to implicitly or explicitly illustrate the nature of the 'choice' people face in a market economy (for example, Howarth 1990; McIntosh 1972). Just as a highwayman ostensibly offers his victims a choice between handing over their money and death but in reality coerces people into handing over their cash, so the market is similarly said to offer workers a choice between employment on terms determined by the economically powerful and poverty, which in reality amounts to being coerced into working for the wealthy. In the words of Olsaretti (1998, p. 71), 'a choice is voluntary if and only if *it is not made because there is no acceptable alternative to it'* and the market frequently fails to provide an acceptable alternative.

An involuntary choice is, of course, no choice at all, but rather describes coercion. Hence, asymmetries of bargaining power are said to lead to what Walzer (1983, p. 102) has termed 'desperate exchanges' in which individuals appear to have little choice but to 'agree' to a harmful, unfair or exploitative exchange. Indeed, an individual's choices may be so limited that they have no plausible alternative but to undertake work that by its very nature constitutes exploitation. Commercial surrogacy and prostitution are the most commonly cited examples of such work; it is widely believed that people who sell their reproductive or sexual labour must do so out of desperation or coercion because it is assumed that people would only undertake such intimate activities in exchange for money if they felt they had no plausible alternative means of earning a living. As Malm (1989, p. 61) has noted, if it is believed that 'Poor women ... may feel compelled to enter these arrangements when they would prefer not to do so' then 'we ought to prohibit the arrangements in order to protect poor women from exploitation.'

Indeed, in Engels' (1968, p. 149) supposedly realistic empirical study of the conditions of the industrial workforce of nineteenth-century England, it was claimed that the power of the capitalists over their employees even extended to the forced prostitution of female mill workers:

> It is, besides, a matter of course that factory servitude, like any other, and to an even higher degree, confers *jus primæ noctis* upon the master. In this respect also the employer is sovereign over the persons and charms of his employees. The threat of discharge suffices to overcome all resistance in nine cases out of ten, if not in ninety-nine out of a hundred, in girls who, in any case, have no strong inducement to chastity.

Given that, according to the logic of Marxist analysis, workers had to accept employment on whatever terms the capitalist offered or face starvation, it followed that for the capitalist, 'his mill is also his harem'. Irrespective of the historical accuracy of Engels' claim, it is certainly true that the view that those who engage in prostitution or commercial surrogacy are the victims of coercion or exploitation remains an important driver of public policy and one reason why such activities are illegal (or exist in a legal grey area) in most liberal democracies.

For many scholars, then, the ethical basis of the market is seriously compromised by the belief that many of the supposedly voluntary exchanges that people undertake in the marketplace are founded upon exploitation and coercion. This chapter will now show that these claims are without foundation as they are based upon a flawed conception of how a real world market economy works and the limits to individual choice that exist in any social situation.

Choice and constraint in the marketplace

Before addressing the systematic and substantive critiques of the market set out immediately above, this section will first deal with the more basic and intuitive critiques described at the outset of the previous section. Here, it was argued that certain practices fundamental to a market economy – using people for one's own ends, profiting from other people's needs and arbitrage – were inherently exploitative.

First, there is no reason why using other people as a means of achieving one's own ends should be deemed inherently exploitative or even wrong. To ask a stranger for directions, for example, is to treat that person as a means of achieving one's end of finding a particular location, but it does not follow that that person has been exploited. Equally, as was elucidated at length in Chapter 2, economic activity in an advanced society requires the coordination of many thousands, if not millions, of people and the only way such an advanced division of labour can be sustained is if people use one another as a means of achieving their own ends by responding to the price signals generated by the market. Prosperity cannot be founded on self-sufficiency, it requires people to serve one another, but that does not mean that they are exploited.

The fact that success in the marketplace is based upon people's ability to satisfy the needs of others is an important component of the ethical case for the market. Profiting from other people's needs is a feature of any economic system in which people receive recompense for providing the goods and services that others want. While some have claimed that a distinction should be drawn between those needs that are properly met in the marketplace and those that are not, it is not clear why it is morally acceptable for supermarkets and farmers to profit from people's need for food, for example, but not for healthcare professionals to profit from people's health needs. Or is it to be suggested that doctors and nurses who do not work for free or for a subsistence wage, are exploiters of the sick and needy? Of course, different individuals do have different health needs through no fault of their own, but in this sense healthcare is simply an example of an insurable risk like many others.

It is not possible to provide for people's needs without in some sense engaging with their vulnerabilities, given that an element of vulnerability is likely to be present in any relationship that concerns needs and desires. As Wood (1995, p. 143) has noted, 'Many human needs and desires can be viewed as vulnerabilities, and accordingly many dealings between human beings can be put in an exploitative light.' The emotional need for love, the physical need for sustenance, and the intellectual need for mental stimulation may all render us in some way vulnerable to people who we believe can satisfy these needs. This does not mean that to seek to provide for people's needs is pernicious or exploitative, though it does mean that those individuals and firms that attempt to do so may be particularly liable to accusations of exploitation.

The sale of insurance, for example, may be cited as a commercial enterprise founded upon the exploitation of people's vulnerability to particular risks, but private insurance provides an important mutually beneficial service that enables people to obtain insurance without the risk being borne by the whole of society. Similarly, a firm that sells burglar alarms to the elderly provides an important service that may reduce the fear of crime and perhaps the likelihood of becoming a victim of crime, while also demonstrating the demand for this service and hence motivating others to entrepreneurially discover new methods of protecting homes.

The exact role of producers in preference-formation will be subject to thorough scrutiny in the following chapter, but it should be noted here that it is extremely paternalistic to suggest that some people are incapable of choosing which goods and services they wish to purchase without being mercilessly exploited by unscrupulous producers. Is it really to be proposed that those products judged to exploit people's vulnerabilities are to be forbidden, or at the very least proscribed to those people deemed vulnerable to exploitation? If so, given the ubiquity of need and vulnerability, and the fact that almost all goods and services sold in the marketplace satisfy needs that are not innate, it is not clear that there are any products that would escape censure under such a scheme. Should novels that exploit our vulnerability for romance, restaurants that exploit our desire for fine food and clothes manufacturers who exploit our desire to look good in order to attract a sexual partner all therefore be prohibited?

The fact that arbitrage is not exploitative is well-known and should not require a great deal of elucidation here. The belief that every physical object has one true value (and that only physical objects can have value) that underlies the perception of arbitrage as morally wrong has been termed 'the physical fallacy' (Sowell 1996, p. 67). As noted in the Chapter 3, it is a basic fact of economics that the value (or marginal utility) of any good or service is not fixed, but varies in different places and at different times and for different people. Hence, a glass of water has a very different marginal utility for a traveller lost in the desert and for a student seated in a lecture theatre. Arbitrage simply reflects this fact and those who profit from it provide an important service by distributing goods to those who value them most highly, thereby contributing to the most efficient use of resources (Miller 1989, pp. 177–8, provides a more detailed discussion with further examples).

Many of the practices fundamental to a market economy may at first sight appear exploitative but are in fact neither harmful nor pernicious, let alone exploitative. Rather, these practices perform an essential function without which a complex, advanced economy could not operate. This section will now turn to the more systematic and substantial critiques of the market as exploitative and coercive.

Monopsony or market?

The systematic critiques of the market as inherently exploitative and coercive described above all characterize the market as a monopsony, where one buyer of labour has such a dominant position in the marketplace that all workers must sell their labour to it. The analogy of the highwayman frequently invoked similarly describes a 'negoti-ation' between two entities without the possibility of third party intervention. In reality, however, a market economy implies a multi-plicity of firms competing for labour; it is inconceivable for even one sector of a market economy to be organized in any other way because of the prohibitive transaction costs that would be created by the existence of one huge monopolistic firm. While one town or city may become highly dependent on one large employer, it nevertheless cannot be accurately described as a monopsony where other firms exist or where people may choose to move to other locations in search of alternative employment.

The existence of multiple firms in the marketplace competing against one another for the most productive workers means that workers are not faced with a stark choice between one fixed wage and unemployment. Rather, workers choose between a multiplicity of occupations in a multiplicity of firms, with the wages determined by the forces of supply and demand. If a firm refuses to match the salaries paid by its competitors, it will suffer the effects of increased employee turnover until it is left with an unproductive workforce who cannot command the higher wages paid elsewhere for whom low wage employment may be the only alternative to unemployment. Such a strategy hardly makes sense for a profit-maximizing firm. It should also be noted that while a 'desperate' unemployed individual may initially accept a low wage or undesirable job, once in employment they are then free to apply to work elsewhere without the urgency or desperation of their initial situation (Murphey 1996, pp. 83–4).

Any example or analogy that describes an employee negotiating with one single employer is fallacious because it does not represent the reality of a market economy, but is more akin to bargaining *in the absence of markets* (Acton 1993, pp. 56–62). It is perhaps ironic that it is the public sectors of contemporary liberal democracies that most closely resemble the caricature of labour market negotiation presented by the critics of the market. In UK healthcare, for example, the National Health Service has a virtual monopsony in employing healthcare professionals. Hence, limiting the scope of the market by extending the public sector will in fact move labour markets closer to the picture of exploitation and coercion depicted by critics of the market.

The accusation that the rewards employees receive in the marketplace may not correspond with their economic contribution or may be below the wage that would be set by a 'perfectly competitive' market economy assumes that there is an objective, correct wage for each occupation, or an objective, correct proportion of a firm's profits that should be paid to its employees. In the real world outside of academic textbooks or formal models, however, there is no such thing as a perfectly competitive economy or an equilibrium wage. Wage rates are the result of the subjective choices of firms and individuals in the marketplace that determine the demand for particular skills and talents, and the willingness of individuals to undertake particular occupations in return for the available rewards. A market wage reflects the value to society of a particular contribution as determined by the impersonal workings of the market.

The assumption that employees have more to lose in negotiations than their employers is also open to question. Contrary to the caricature of the all-powerful business-owner who can exist indefinitely without one additional employee while the worker faces destitution if they are not employed immediately, in reality businesses risk failure and bankruptcy if they do not fulfil orders on time. While short or medium term unemployment is undoubtedly unpleasant (here I write from experience), it may not be as lastingly catastrophic as the complete loss of one's livelihood, assets and ability to raise future capital that can occur in the event of a business failure.

The social limits of choice

It is of course the case that the choices available to any individual in any social context are inevitably constrained by the choices other people make. Nozick (1974, pp. 262–4) illustrated this fact with the example of a hypothetical situation in which twenty-six men and twenty-six women wish to marry a member of the opposite sex. All members of each sex agree on a ranking of the desirability as marriage partners of each member of the opposite sex, ranking the men from A to Z and the women from A^1 and Z^1 in decreasing preferential order. Man A and woman A^1 decide to marry, a decision that deprives all the others of their most preferred partner (A and A^1). B and B^1 then decide to marry, both choosing their second most preferred option. This decision, however, is not made involuntarily simply because there is another choice that both would have preferred. This most preferred option required the cooperation of others (A and A^1) that has been legitimately withheld. If all the remaining individuals decide to marry in accordance with their desirability ranking, so that C marries C^1, and D marries D^1 and so on, then finally Z and Z^1 will be left with the choice of either marrying their least desirable marriage partner or not marrying at all. If Z and Z^1 do decide to marry, the fact that their only alternative to marrying each other (remaining single) was a much worse option and that there were many preferable options (marrying any of A to Y or A^1 and Y^1, respectively) that were made unavailable to them by the actions of others, does not render their marriage an involuntary or coerced act.

Similarly, in any society where people are not sustained by manna from heaven but must work for their subsistence people must inevitably undertake activity that involves personal costs – assuming that they prefer leisure to work. There are, as Wertheimer (1992, p. 215) has described, 'negative *elements* in virtually all employment contracts, indeed, in virtually all uncontroversially beneficial transactions', but, 'We do not say that a worker is harmed by employment...We assume that the benefits that the worker receives from employment are greater than the costs.'

Hence, to show that an individual has been compelled by their economic circumstances to carry out action that they would prefer not to undertake, or that involves personal costs, does not demonstrate that that person has been exploited or coerced, but that other more desirable alternatives required the cooperation of others, for example, people to work to provide one's subsistence while one enjoys leisure, that has been legitimately witheld.

The salient question, following Wertheimer (1992), is not whether those exchanges deemed to be exploitative or coercive involve harm, but whether they constitute a net harm. While the costs and benefits of different courses of action must ultimately be a personal judgement of each individual, one of the characteristic features of such exchanges is that those people who are deemed to be exploited or coerced have, by definition, a great deal to gain from the transaction: 'It is precisely because the exploitee stands to gain so much from the transaction (relative to the exploiter) that his bargaining position is comparatively weak' (Wertheimer 1992, p. 223).

A person said to be exploited or coerced by a more economically powerful entity must be in a position to gain from the exchange. Hence, when a multinational company locates part of its operations to a developing nation in order to attract workers it must offer a wage that will provide a standard of living higher than they could otherwise attain. While the wage rate paid is unlikely to bear comparison with that earned by the firm's employees in the developed world, it constitutes a net gain for its employees and this is why it is able to recruit staff, rather than via coercion or exploitation.

In every society there are jobs that are particularly unpleasant or involve a high degree of risk. The fact that such work tends to bring unusually high monetary rewards provides one means for people to earn a high income. It is inevitable that most of the people attracted to such work will be those who are unable to earn similar rewards from less hazardous or unpleasant occupations and who therefore have the most to gain from such employment.

A qualified doctor who can expect to earn a high salary from medicine is unlikely to be attracted to military service or work on an oil rig, just as commercial surrogacy is unlikely to appeal to a practising barrister. This does not mean, however, that the people who do make such choices are exploited or coerced. Contrary to Hobhouse's equation of the position of adult men and women in the free market with that of the 'helpless child', a market economy is *not* populated by helpless children incapable of making rational choices without being exploited or coerced by capitalist ogres, but is peopled by adult individuals with the ability to choose between the different alternatives that are presented to them as a result of the legitimate choices made by other adults.

It is also perfectly legitimate in the marketplace (as in other social situations) for people to set the terms and conditions upon which they will engage with other people. As Hayek (1960, pp. 135–6) noted, it is entirely appropriate that 'The benefits and opportunities which our fellows offer to us will be available only if we satisfy their conditions.' Just as a hostess may only invite a person to her parties if they conform to her standards of conduct and dress or an individual may wish to converse with their neighbours only if they observe conventional manners, so it is legitimate for a firm to require that its employees dress in a certain way or agree to a particular code of conduct. This is an important part of the heuristic process by which the market enables individuals to learn about the needs and expectations of others and requires them to adjust their behaviour accordingly if they are to achieve their own goals. It is for this reason, for example, that a sixteen-year-old with no formal qualifications or work experience must learn to behave in accordance with the demands of potential employees, which are in turn driven by the demands of consumers and may involve dressing or acting in certain ways or acquiring further training or education.

The fact that people's choices in the marketplace are limited does not mean that they are exploited or coerced. As noted in Chapter 2, a woman may wish to be a world famous supermodel but has to accept a less desirable alternative until and unless she can convince other people that she has the skills and attributes necessary for a career on the catwalk. If she accepts a job in a supermarket this does not mean that she has been exploited or coerced, but is indicative of the fact that in any social situation we must all redraw and revise our plans and aspirations in the context of the plans and aspirations of others. What the market does provide, however, are price signals that act as a guide as to how we should amend our behaviour if we are to come close to realizing our plans and aspirations.

The surplus and the role of the entrepreneur

The Marxist view of capitalist exploitation as involving the confiscation by the capitalist of the value produced by the worker – irrespective of whether it is labour that produces value – is a perfect example of the 'physical fallacy': the belief that only physical products or physical labour can add or constitute value. According to this view, a successful capitalist entrepreneur such as the founder and owner of the Virgin group Richard Branson owes his fortune solely to his ability to extract large amounts of surplus from the products created by his employees. In reality, entrepreneurs such as Branson are not parasites living off the blood of their workers. Rather, it is the entrepreneur who makes the crucial contribution to the economic success of their business.

Entrepreneurs perform a role in the management and organization of their businesses and therefore of the economy as a whole. Even a socialist economy would require management and organization and those who performed such a role – presumably the members of the central planning board – would have to be paid. While the application of managerial and organizational skills does not produce a physical product in the same sense as carpentry or bricklaying, it nevertheless adds value to the economy. The decision to develop one idea and not another, to invest in one design rather than an alternative or to employ a particular individual in a particular role are examples of seemingly ephemeral decisions that in fact add genuine economic value.

As Schumpeter (1943, p. 132) noted, business entrepreneurs play a crucial role in a dynamic market economy that 'does not essentially consist in either inventing anything or otherwise creating the conditions which the enterprise exploits', but rather involves innovation, overcoming resistance to change, and, in short, 'getting things done'. Hence, while Richard Branson does not perform the music sold by the Virgin record label nor pilot the planes flown by the Virgin airline, it can nevertheless be argued that his creative contribution has been the critical factor in the success of the Virgin group.

Entrepreneurs also perform an important role by investing in new business ventures, an activity that often involves a high level of risk and requires a willingness to wait for a return on one's capital. Those who invest in a new business risk losing their investment, while although the workers they employ may face unemployment should the business fail, they will not be required to pay back a portion of their salary. As Nozick (1974, p. 256) has described, the division between employers and employees within a market economy has allowed the workforce to divest themselves of the risks inherent in entrepreneurial activity. In a society without such a division, either every individual would be required to share the risks of the particular enterprise in which they worked or all would be required to share the losses resulting from poor investment decisions (which would be numerous given the epistemic pathologies of such a system).

Rather than being non-productive scroungers consuming the value produced by other people, capitalist entrepreneurs undertake a positive function that must be performed in every successful advanced economy, market or non-market.

Moreover, the distinction between capitalists and workers drawn by those scholars working within the Marxist tradition bears little resemblance to the reality of contemporary market economies. Today, many people may be employees of a firm for a number of years before starting their own business with capital saved or borrowed, hence (in Marxist terms) moving from the proletariat to the bourgeoisie. Equally, many employees are also shareholders in their own and other firms – for example, in 2005 more than 100,000 of the 237,000 employees of UK supermarket Tesco owned shares in the company – therefore simultaneously being capitalists and workers. Many of the most highly paid managers are employees, working for a fixed annual salary, making them, according to Marxist doctrine, wage-slaves exploited by the capitalist class. During the course of a lifetime any one individual may be an employee, employer and self-employed at different times.

Conclusion

The efficiency and prosperity gains that result from market mechanisms mean that a market economy offers people a wider range of choices than those available in any other economic system. While no economic system can give people the 'right' to do whatever they want, a market economy does furnish people with a myriad of different alternatives that are barely imaginable to people living in non-market economies. A market economy is not a monopsony where one desperate worker negotiates with one all-powerful employer – a 'your money or your life' situation – but is made up of a multiplicity of different firms offering a multiplicity of different opportunities. Those who enter into contracts that some deem inherently exploitative or coercive are in fact exercising their right as adults to reap the often substantial rewards that come from engaging in activities that others consider morally objectionable. In the case of prostitution, for example, Satz (1995, p. 66) has noted that both male and female prostitutes tend to be drawn from across the whole socio-economic spectrum, suggesting that such a choice is the result of a rational assessment of the personal costs and benefits involved.

There are, of course, some exchanges (and hence occupations) that are properly outlawed in a market economy, though not, it must be stressed, on the grounds that they constitute exploitation or coercion. It is not permissible, for example, to pay someone to harm another person (against that person's wishes). Thus, even if a psychopath actively wanted to be a paid hitman, would clearly derive tremendous pleasure from such work and was willing to perform it for a subsistence salary, it would still be wrong to employ them to do so because it is not legitimate to murder or injury other people. Commercial surrogacy may also be considered an illegitimate exchange, though, again, not on the grounds of exploitation or coercion, but because it involves the sale of a human being (the baby) and it is not possible to own and therefore to sell another person.[1] Similarly, health and safety regulations are a legitimate feature of the marketplace, not to prevent exploitation or coercion, but to prevent people being harmed as a result of ignorance, carelessness or stupidity on the part of either the employer or employee. It is worth noting, however, that wherever possible self-regulation is preferable to external regulation because those familiar with particular industries are more likely to have knowledge of the risks involved than those with little direct experience of the relevant working practices.

The arguments advanced in this chapter lead to the conclusion that policies such as minimum wage legislation and the prohibition of occupations like prostitution are not justified on the grounds of the prevention of exploitation or coercion. Paradoxically, such policies limit the choices available to individuals and are liable to harm those they are intended to help. There is compelling evidence that minimum wage laws increase unemployment among the low skilled, denying a first foot on the employment ladder to those who need it most (for example, Bartlett 2000), while the outlawing of prostitution criminalizes a profession that offers many men and women the opportunity to earn substantially more than they could realistically hope to receive in alternative occupations.

The more the public sector encroaches on the private sector and each industry and profession comes to be dominated by one single government enterprise, the more the economy takes on the characteristics of the monopsony that so many critics of the market allege places employees in a situation where they are exposed to exploitation and coercion by employers. An economy free from the spectre of exploitation and coercion will be one in which the market is given free reign to develop a myriad of competing sources of economic power and each individual has the greatest possible freedom to exit from those transactions that they do not wish to participate in.

Note

1. This objection to commercial surrogacy may be overcome if surrogacy is deemed to involve the sale of parenting rights to a particular child, rather than the sale of the child himself or herself, though the validity of this distinction cannot be resolved here (see Alexander and O'Driscoll 1980; Anderson 1990).

6
Culture and Well-being

The efficiency achieved by the market means that it is able to satisfy more needs and preferences than any comparable economic system, but it may not necessarily follow that this will lead to an increase in the sum total of human happiness. Critics of the market have argued that it is an institutional setting that leads people to frame their needs and preferences in terms of self-centred, myopic and hedonistic choices that create a 'dumbed-down', 'lowest common denominator' culture incongruent with human well-being. For this reason it is argued that the scope of the market should be limited to protect those social and cultural practices that are essential to well-being and that will be under-supplied by the market.

The impact of the market on well-being is central to an ethical assessment of the market: if it can be shown that in the marketplace individual choices are structured in such a way that people consistently select alternatives incongruent with their own happiness and contentment then the ethical basis of the market must be questioned.

Lane (1991, p. 3) has argued that economic efficiency is the wrong yardstick by which to measure the success of the market because it neglects the impact of the market on well-being:

> [T]he market should be judged by the satisfactions people receive as a consequence of their market experiences and by what they learn from them. I would substitute these criteria for the current criteria: efficiency in producing and distributing goods and services.

It is argued that the market should be judged in terms of its overall contribution to human well-being – measured here in terms of the experiences and satisfactions that people receive from participating in the market – rather than according to its ability to produce and distribute an ever-increasing quantity of goods and services.

Plan of the chapter

This chapter will begin by setting out this critique of the market as an institutional setting in which people make narrow, selfish, myopic choices as 'consumers', as opposed to the altruistic, sustainable, other-regarding choices that people make as 'citizens' in democratic and deliberative forums. Consequently, in the marketplace many people find themselves trapped on a 'hedonic treadmill' of work to fund consumption that does not lead to the hoped for contentment, while the choices that would bring happiness are closed-off by the institutional setting of the market.

Having set out this cultural and moral critique of the market, this chapter will then present the counter-argument that will show that the depiction of decision-making in the marketplace provided by the critics of the market presents a completely erroneous view of the market process. The critics of economic growth as an end also neglect the enormous benefits that come from material prosperity. It will also be noted that where the market is excluded from the supply of many non-material goods and services, then the market will inevitably appear to be materialistic because it supplies predominately material goods. Finally, this chapter will show that the market does not produce a 'lowest common denominator' culture in which the most base and shallow cultural products predominate, but creates a wide array of cultural products from the very highest to the very lowest forms.

Choice and the citizen-consumer dichotomy

The belief that market mechanisms may impose negative externalities on the well-being of many members of commercial society can be traced back to the earliest writings on market exchange and, indeed, to one of the market's staunchest defenders. Adam Smith expressed profound concern about the impact of an advanced division of labour – the basis of commercial society – on those members of the workforce who would be required to undertake the most monotonous and unrewarding work. In *The Wealth of Nations*, Smith (1981, p. 782) wrote: 'The man whose whole life is spent performing a few simple operations', having little opportunity to exert his intelligence, 'naturally loses, therefore, the habit of such exertion, and generally becomes as stupid and as ignorant as it is possible for a human creature to become'. Smith believed that as an economy advanced and the division of labour became more profound, greater numbers of people would find their working lives reduced to the repetition of one small task, with resultant negative consequences for their morale and well-being.[1]

Adam Smith's description of the fate of many people employed within an advanced division of labour was clearly overly pessimistic; it is empirically not the case that the great majority of the workforce now find their working lives reduced to the performance of one or two simple tasks. In fact, on the contrary, the development of market economies has created far greater opportunities for interesting and fulfilling work than have existed at any time in the past or in any alternative economic system. Hence, this aspect of Smith's work should be read more as a critique of the changing nature of work during the process of industrialization than of market economies *per se* (Wilson 1995, pp. 47–8).

Nevertheless, Smith's depiction of the unfortunates whose lives had been ruined by the soul-destroying nature of their daily work remains rhetorically powerful to this day because it connects with a long-standing moral and cultural critique of the market. This critique sees the marketplace as an institutional setting where people surrender their well-being to soul-destroying work so as to gain the material rewards that such work brings, but these rewards do not adequately compensate for the loss of well-being that was required to attain them.

In contemporary scholarship, the choices that individuals make within the institutional context of the market are often contrasted with the choices that they make within the institutional framework of democratic decision-making. It is argued that in the marketplace individuals make narrow, self-interested choices as 'consumers', whereas, by contrast, within democratic forums individuals make reflective, altruistic choices as 'citizens'. The market, it is argued, feeds people's 'lower nature', which is governed by subconscious desires that respond to external stimuli, and bypasses their 'higher nature', which is based upon deliberate, conscious decision-making informed by logic and calculation. Consumers, it is argued, choose instant-gratification and convenience over quality and integrity; they choose fast food, trash television and pop music over haute cuisine, literature and classical music. Given that individual needs and wants are contingent upon what they experience and what they see others experiencing, if the market is allowed free rein it is argued that this 'lowest common denominator' culture will become endemic. Hence, if producers respond uncritically to the preferences expressed by consumers in the marketplace, though there may be some fleeting pleasures, the long-term consequence will be the diminution of well-being rather than the attainment of the good life (Barber 1984; Buckley and Casson 2001; Frank 1999; Knight 1997; Sagoff 1988; Sunstein 1991).

The alleged distinction between consumer and citizen choices has been articulated by a number of communitarian and democratic theorists. Barber (1984, p. 22), for example, has described the consumer as 'a greedy, self-interested, acquisitive survivor' whose actions are geared towards achieving 'ultimate material satisfaction'. The consumer, it is alleged, 'uses the gift of choice to multiply his options in and to transform the material conditions of the world, but never to transform himself or to create a world of mutuality with his fellow humans'. The consumer, then, is the *homo economicus* of neo-classical economics, hedonistically seeking to maximize his utility without regard to the externalities that are imposed on others by his actions. Citizens, by contrast, 'are neighbours bound together neither by blood nor by contract but by their common concerns and common participation in the search for common solutions to common problems' (Barber 1984, p. 219).

Sagoff (1988) has illustrated the consumer–citizen divide with the example of an experiment he conducted that involved testing his students' responses to the development of a ski resort on environmentally sensitive national park land. When asked whether they would visit the resort to make use of its amenities, the majority of his students enthusiastically assented. When asked whether the development of the national park should be given planning approval, however, the response was almost unanimously negative. For Sagoff (1988, p. 51), these apparently contradictory opinions illustrate the conflict 'between what the students as individuals wanted for themselves and what they thought we should do, collectively, as a nation'. It is argued that when the students approached the proposal as consumers they wanted to take advantage of the opportunities for recreation offered by the development of the new ski resort, but when they judged the proposal as citizens they valued the preservation of the unspoilt natural environment more highly.[2]

Sagoff (1988, pp. 52–3) further illustrated the consumer–citizen dichotomy with examples from his own life:

> Last year, I bribed a judge to fix a couple of traffic tickets and I was glad to do so because I saved my licence. Yet, at election time, I helped to vote the corrupt judge out of office . . . I love my car; I hate the bus. Yet I vote for candidates who promise to tax gasoline to pay for public transportation.

Sagoff's contention, then, is that in the marketplace we act as self-interested consumers: bribing officials, using environmentally unfriendly modes of transport. In the political sphere, however, we act as public-spirited citizens: voting out corrupt officials, supporting environmentally friendly transport policies. According to Sagoff (1988, p. 53), the political causes he supports have little or no basis in his interests as a consumer, 'because I take different points of view when I vote and when I shop'.

It is contended that people behave as consumers in the marketplace and citizens in the political sphere because participation in democratic processes provides an opportunity to learn about the preferences and values of others that is absent from a market context. According to Barber (1984, p. 224), 'it is as a citizen that the individual confronts the Other and adjusts his own life plans to the dictates of a shared world'. When individuals come together as citizens, rather than acting as isolated consumers, it is argued that a process of 'self-transformation' can take place, whereby, in the words of Warren (1992, p. 8), individuals 'become more public-spirited, more tolerant, more knowledgeable, more attentive to the interests of others, and more probing of their own interests'. Hence, whereas the market simply responds to individual preferences, albeit very effectively, it is argued that democratic institutions allow for reflection on and learning from the standpoints and opinions of others, and this enables participants to transform their self-regarding consumer preferences into other-regarding citizen values.

Consumerism and the 'hedonic treadmill'

It is contended, then, that the market structures individual choices so as to produce a materialistic culture in which individuals form preferences for consumer goods that bring only fleeting satisfaction, environmental resources are depleted with little regard to the future and superficial cultural products are produced in abundance, crowding out more challenging and enduring alternatives.

Lane (1991, 1998) has argued that those who live and work in an advanced market economy have become trapped on a 'hedonic treadmill', where they believe that more income will make them happy, but when their income does rise they continue to be dissatisfied, while still retaining the belief that a further rise in income will bring happiness.

The metaphor of the helpless consumer running on a treadmill of endless work in order to fund endless consumption is one that reoccurs throughout the literature that is critical of the link between the material prosperity generated by the market and well-being. Galbraith (1999, p. 125) compared those who would defend the market on the grounds that it effectively satisfies the needs of consumers to 'the onlooker who applauds the efforts of the squirrel to keep abreast of the wheel that is propelled by his own efforts'. Wachtel (1983, p. 79) evoked a similar image in his critique of 'the poverty of affluence':

> Our overriding stress on growth and productivity and the toll it takes on our health and well-being are part of a tragically unnecessary treadmill on which we run, ever more desperately, with ever more strain, committing more and more of our lives to the hopeless chase to keep up.

According to Wachtel (1983, pp. 3–4), within a market economy, 'people really do experience a need for the things that they buy' but 'the experience of economic needs in our culture is an artifact of how we *have* set things up'.

It is contended that the needs satisfied by a market economy do not bring fulfilment because they are not genuine needs, but 'needs' manufactured by the economy itself. The process of production itself creates the desire for consumer goods such as silk shirts, kitchenware and widescreen televisions. According to Galbraith (1999, p. 127), within a market economy, advertising and salesmanship 'bring into being wants that did not previously exist'. The insatiable consumer demand for new products can be attributed to the vast sums of money that producers spend every year persuading consumers that they 'need' their products. Lasch (1978, p. 72) has argued that 'the consumer, perpetually unsatisfied, restless, anxious, and bored' is a creation of the advertising industry. Advertising not only 'upholds consumption as the answer to the age-old discontents of loneliness, sickness, weariness, lack of sexual satisfaction', it also 'creates new forms of discontent peculiar to the modern age' (Lasch 1978, p. 72). Advertising, it is alleged, creates a yearning for consumer goods on the promise that the consumption of such products will bring happiness and contentment. It undermines people's self-control by pandering to their 'lower nature' that craves immediate gratification (Buckley and Casson 2001).

The culture of the market, it is argued, reflects and perpetuates this shallow materialism, crowding out the opportunity for the creation of more challenging and transformative cultural products. In the words of Keat (2000, p. 158):

> Television 'ratings wars' provide plentiful examples, with programmes carefully constructed to provide audiences with 'just what they (happen to) want', forcing out others which, by virtue of their transformative value, present something to their audiences which may challenge those preferences.

Individuals socialized within market society lack the experience or the education that would lead them to demand more challenging cultural products. According to Scitovsky (1992, p. 225), 'all stimulus enjoyment is skilled consumption'. That is, lasting pleasure requires the investment of the time and effort necessary to appreciate the nuances and intricacies of a particular activity. The enjoyment of classical music, for example, is a learned ability rather than an innate talent. Similarly, full appreciation of chess, football or bullfighting will also require an education in the activity's subtleties. According to Scitovsky (1992, p. viii), the citizens of market economies live lives of boredom and dissatisfaction because without an appropriate cultural education they are incapable of making truly rewarding choices: 'Advancing civilization would advance our happiness if our education for enjoying leisure by putting it to good use increased in step with the increase in our leisure.'

By satisfying our most immediate wants and providing little incentive or opportunity to learn and to reframe our desires in the light of the experiences of others, it is claimed that the market has a cultural deskilling effect that ultimately undermines the well-being of the inhabitants of commercial society. Indeed, it is alleged that consumerism is all-pervasive within a market economy to the extent that even the political 'radicals' of the 1960s who sought to replace the ideology of consumerism with new forms of social, economic and political relationships have found themselves living lives not dissimilar to those of their parents that they had wanted to reject (Wachtel 1983, Chapter 8).

Materialism, it is contended, cannot deliver on its promise of happiness and fulfilment: the satisfaction of needs that are not genuine cannot lead to well-being, but can only lead to the formation of new 'needs' still to be satisfied. Consequently, life within an affluent market economy becomes a seemingly inescapable cycle of desire, work, purchase and disappointment. Hence, it is claimed that the 'freedom' of capitalist society is in fact 'repressive': while individuals ostensibly enjoy freedom of choice in the marketplace, in reality their choices are limited to alternatives that cannot bring genuine fulfilment (Marcuse 1968).

It is argued, then, that the material prosperity that results from the efficiency of the market does not produce a corresponding improvement in well-being. While material prosperity could have freed people from a life of endless toil, it has instead led to the creation of a 'hedonic treadmill' upon which the vast majority of the population are trapped. Individuals work to fund their desire for more consumer goods in the mistaken belief that those goods will bring the fulfilment that their lives lack. When the happiness from one purchase proves short-lived, the only choice that appears to be available is to work to fund the next purchase in the hope that it might prove more satisfying. Consumerism drives the motor of economic growth, but it also traps the population of a market economy in an emotionally impoverished state by structuring their choices so that happiness appears to be something that can be brought in the high street or in the supermarket with no possibility of any alternative way of life. According to Lane (1998, p. 461), 'markets create a market culture that guides (I would say misguides) the pursuit of happiness', leading people to make choices that are incongruent with their own well-being.

Choice and well-being in the marketplace

All individual choices are to a large degree determined by the context in which they are made. Indeed, a large part of every individual's personality is contingent upon the cultural context in which they are socialized. As noted in the previous chapter, any need, desire or taste, beyond the most basic needs for food, shelter and sex, are to a very great extent socially contingent. As Hayek (1967b, p. 315) described, 'the tastes of man, as is also true of his opinions and beliefs and indeed much of his personality, are shaped in great measure by his cultural environment'. Or, as the contemporary political philosopher Richard Rorty (1989, p. 177) has put it, somewhat more starkly (and with some exaggeration): 'There is nothing to people except what has been socialized into them . . . It is a historical contingency whether we are socialized by Neanderthals, ancient Chinese, Eton, Summerhill or the Ministry of Truth.'

The enjoyment of literature, orange squash or fine wine, for example, are all contingent upon the membership of a society in which such goods and services are produced. Had Ernest Hemingway never written a single novel, for example, people would not experience an innate desire to read his work. Similarly, had orange squash never been produced, people would likewise not experience an innate craving for this drink. Hence, people do not spontaneously start playing rock music without first coming into contact with this particular type of music nor do they spontaneously decide to wear a suit and tie to work unless they see others dressed this way. Needs, tastes and preferences are formed via an evolutionary social process characterized by innovation and imitation (Hayek 1967b).

Given that individual preferences are contingent upon the available experiences and choices, the context in which preferences are formed is all important. However, the contention that individuals make selfish, myopic choices as consumers in the marketplace and altruistic, public-spirited choices as democratic citizens is based upon an erroneous conception of the decision-making process that exists in each institutional context. Choices made within the institutional framework of the market are not solitary, atomistic choices made without reference to the needs and values of others. On the contrary, as set out at length in Chapter 2, the market is a process founded upon heuristic learning about other people's needs and values. If individuals are to realize their ends within the institutional framework of the market, irrespective of whether those ends are altruistic or self-interested, they *must take into account the needs and values of others* that are communicated by the price signals generated by the market.

When producers and consumers respond to the price signals generated by the market, they respond to the myriad of different needs and preferences that those prices represent. Whereas an individual can only consciously comprehend the needs and preferences of a limited number of known individuals, the market process enables each individual to learn about the needs and preferences of a practically infinite number of people dispersed throughout the economy. Hence, the institutional setting of the market requires each individual to take into account the needs and preferences of a greater number of people than is possible in a democratic forum where the needs and preferences of others that *can* be taken into account will be limited by what any one individual can intellectually comprehend.

Consumer choices are not only taken in the context of the needs and preferences of others, they are also costed choices that must reflect the trade-offs that have to be made between alternative uses of finite resources. As noted in Chapter 3, when people purchase goods and services in the marketplace, they must choose between different uses of the resources at their disposal. The decision to buy a new fridge rather than to take an expensive foreign holiday, or to purchase a new car rather than a gym membership are trade-offs between alternative uses of resources. The knowledge that a person cannot have a new fridge and an exotic holiday, or a new car and a gym membership, forces them to order the alternatives according to their relative and subjective importance. It is only in this act of choosing, in the act of actually making pecuniary trade-offs, that knowledge of an individual's true preferences may be revealed. While an individual may believe that they know their personal preferences intimately, it may be that only when the act of choosing actually takes place and sacrifices must be made that such information will be fully revealed (Sowell 1996, pp. 217–18).

By contrast, choices that individuals make in the democratic process are not similarly costed: the costs involved may not be transparent, may be indirect and dispersed among a large number of people. Hence, in the democratic process individuals are liable to vote in favour of a particular regime of education or healthcare provision, for example, that does not reflect their genuine preferences that would emerge if direct costs were attached to each option. Similarly, when individuals are asked to choose between alternatives in an opinion poll survey they may choose an ideal option because they are not required to sacrifice other uses of their resources to meet the cost. Hence, while people's responses in surveys may suggest that they are unhappy with the alternatives offered to them in the marketplace, there is good reason to privilege the choices that people actually make in the marketplace over the results of such opinion polls because it is only the choices that people make in the marketplace that are properly costed and hence reflect the trade-offs and sacrifices that people are actually willing to make (Pennington 2003b).

In the marketplace, then, choices must be made in the context of the needs, values and preferences of others, and in the light of the costs and trade-offs that are attached to different uses of the resources at our disposal. Furthermore, the market communicates that frequently tacit information that can be revealed only in the act of choosing.

There is also strong evidence that people's conduct in different institutional contexts does not fit Sagoff's narrow categorization between self-interest in the marketplace and altruism in democratic forums. Today, supermarkets shelves are stocked with 'environmentally friendly' washing powders, 'dolphin friendly' tins of tuna fish and 'fair trade' coffee that aim to appeal to the 'ethical consumer'. There have also been a number of successful consumer boycotts of specific products on ethical grounds, such as the international boycotts of businesses that invested in the South African Apartheid regime in the 1980s, and the boycott of French wine in response to that country's testing of nuclear weapons in the Pacific in the 1990s. Equally, numerous studies of voting behaviour have demonstrated the importance of the electorate's perception of their own personal economic prospects under alternative manifestos – the so-called 'feel-good' factor – in determining how people vote (for example, Pissarides 1980; Sanders 1999). People clearly do take their other-regarding values into the marketplace and are very often motivated by self-interest when they enter the ballot box. It is naïve to suggest that people do not allow other-regarding values to inform their choices as consumers, or that self-interested concerns do not influence the decisions people make as democratic citizens (see also Meadowcroft 2005).

The needs satisfied by a market economy arise from a process of inter-subjective learning between consumers and producers. Contrary to the caricature of the helpless consumer who has little choice but to purchase the latest product that they see advertised, the vast majority of new consumer brands fail and most of those that do succeed replace existing products in the marketplace. Consumers do not respond to advertisements in the manner of helpless automatons, obliged to buy each new product they see promoted, but are able to assess the likely costs and benefits of new innovations against their existing preferences. If consumers really were as susceptible to advertising as is sometimes claimed, then no business would ever go bankrupt and no new product would ever fail. Rather than deceiving or misleading consumers, advertising plays a crucial role in providing people with information about the potential pros and cons of new and existing products. Successful advertising, by building sales of a product, also contributes to the reduction of the unit costs of production, thus making possible price reductions for consumers (Davidson 1976; Harris and Seldon 1959; Lebergott 1993, Chapter 3; Mises 1996, pp. 320–2).

Growth, prosperity and well-being

The choices that individuals make in the marketplace demonstrate that for the vast majority of people the benefits of increased economic growth, prosperity and consumption outweigh the costs.

The citizens of market economies have consistently chosen a higher material standard of living over other uses of the resources generated by prosperity, while patterns of global migration show that many people in poor non-market societies choose the lifestyle offered by market economies when given such a choice. Furthermore migrants to capitalist countries make a choice about what sort of society they wish to live in order to maximize their well-being before becoming 'addicted' to the consumption of material goods or socialized into a materialistic lifestyle; it cannot be said that they only value this way of life because they have never experienced an alternative.

Economic prosperity brings obvious benefits of increased access to consumer goods and a higher material standard of living. Many of these goods, such as designer jeans and personal stereos, may seem little more than superficial luxuries, but the value that people place on such seeming superficiality should not be underestimated. Postrel (2003, p. ix) recounts how after the fall of the Afghan Taliban regime that had outlawed all consumer goods, from televisions to nail varnish:

> [A] Michigan hairdresser went to Kabul with a group of doctors, nurses, dentists, and social workers...to serve as an all-purpose assistant to the relief mission's professionals...[but] found her own services every bit as popular as the serious business of health and welfare.

After their liberation, many of the people who had been subjected to such a brutally oppressive and destructive regime desired the luxury of professional hairdressing as much as the necessity of professional medical care.

It is also the case that many consumer goods, such as automatic washing machines and vacuum cleaners, are labour saving devices that have made a genuine impact on the quality of life, particularly for women who have been traditionally required to undertake the majority of household tasks that these devices make easier. Adam Smith was wrong when he foresaw that a market economy would condemn a large proportion of the world to monotonous labour; in fact, it is economic growth driven by the market that has freed an unprecedented number of people from domestic drudgery.

Economic growth also brings increased life expectancy and better health during that lifetime as a result of better nutrition and increased access to high quality healthcare. Growth also leads to improved education, which may open the door to further prosperity and to personal and intellectual development. In short, the wealthier a society is, the more resources its members can devote to healthcare and to education (see Boettke 2001, pp. 276–84; Goklany 2002; Haines 1995; Hill 1995; Norberg 2001, Chapters 1 and 2; Preston 1995).

Increased leisure time is another benefit that follows from economic growth. In the United States, for example, the average working week has shortened by half in the last century and a half, from an average of seventy hours in 1850 to between forty and thirty-five hours a week now. Comparable changes have taken place in all other developed nations (Galbraith 1999, p. 243; see also Robinson 1995). As Lane (1991, p. 544) has noted: 'Over the past fifty years the people in market economies have taken much of their new wealth in leisure – almost as much as they have taken in goods.' There is no evidence to support Cohen's (1977) claim that capitalist economies have an in-built tendency to increase output at the expense of increased leisure time. The empirical reality of the vast expansion of leisure time as market economies develop contradicts the claim that the populations of these societies are trapped on a treadmill of endless labour.

The benefits of economic growth described above do not stop accruing once a certain point in development has been reached. Continued gains in life expectancy, access to healthcare and educa-tion, increased leisure time, freedom from domestic drudgery and monotonous labour are made with each developmental step forward. Conversely, it is also the case that the economic dysfunction inherent in the creation of a non-market economy tends to reverse many of the same gains. Those countries that adopted planned non-market economies during the twentieth century witnessed dramatic (absolute and relative) declines in almost all measures of well-being during that period (Henderson 2004).

Having said that, it is not the case that every citizen of contemporary market economies values the material benefits of continued economic growth more than alternative ways of life. The growth of (what has become known as) 'post-materialism' in the most economically advanced countries of the world in recent decades (for example Inglehart 1996) demonstrates that some people (rightly or wrongly) do not accept the premise that continued economic growth is necessarily a good thing. The development of post-materialism demonstrates that people are capable of making an informed choice as to whether or not to participate in the mainstream culture of commercial society. Post-materialism should also be seen as part of the competitive market process in which people spontaneously develop and pursue new ways of living that if deemed successful will be imitated by other people; post-materialism is no more counter to the market process than the growth of organic farming or the development of tabloid size quality newspapers. Such innovation, imitation and heuristic learning are all characteristics of the market process that constantly expands consumer choice (Pennington 2003b). Nevertheless, it should be noted that those people who do opt-out of capitalist societies in order to choose 'simpler' lifestyles tend to do so only after first accumulating sufficient capital to enable themselves to continue to enjoy the material standard of living to which they have become accustomed.

Materialism, non-materialism and 'addiction'

It is of course the case that where the market is restricted to the provision of material goods for immediate consumption it will inevitably appear to be a materialistic mechanism that caters only for the short-term gratification of people's most base desires. The fact that non-material goods and services such as healthcare and education may be provided by the market is obscured by the fact that markets are frequently prevented or crowded out from the provision of these very goods and services by government intervention.

Those who accuse the market of simply responding to myopic, hedonistic preferences appear blind to the fact that markets can and do provide such wide-ranging goods and services as insurance, healthcare, schooling, housing, transport infrastructure (for example, almost all London's underground railway lines were originally built and operated by private companies), health clubs and international air travel. It is simply incorrect to suggest that markets only cater to 'dumbed-down' or materialistic preferences; markets can and do supply goods and services to meet the whole gamut of human wants and needs.

It may be true that in the marketplace some individuals do become 'addicted' to the pursuit of material possessions that do not bring lasting happiness, but it is similarly true that individuals may become 'addicted' to sexual activities that do not bring spiritual fulfilment or to the pursuit of educational qualifications that likewise do not lead to the anticipated increase in well-being. People may be 'trapped' by material *and non-material* choices that do not bring the expected returns of happiness and fulfilment, but this does not mean that such choices are illegitimate or should be prohibited. Rather, it is important that individuals take responsibility for their own actions and have the opportunity to learn from their mistakes, something that can only occur where individuals are free to make their own choices instead of having their decisions made for them by people who believe they know better.

If the market does have the extraordinary power to structure people's choices in the way that so many of its critics claim, then surely this is an argument for extending the scope of the market to the supply of non-material goods and services, such as healthcare and education, so that people will be led by the power of the market to spend their resources on these services rather than on the material goods that the critics of the market so clearly disapprove of. In this sense, the critique of the market outlined earlier in this chapter may be self-defeating because it logically leads to an argument for extending the scope of the market as far as possible into the provision of non-material goods and services.

Culture in the marketplace

The market is a process through which individuals learn about the needs and preferences of others. The fact that profits can be made from supplying a particular good or service provides information about the demand for that product and hence about the needs and preferences of other people. The belief that a market in cultural products will inevitably lead to cultural decline, and that therefore public authorities should intervene in order to evaluate and regulate cultural products, dates back to the origins of commercial society and the emergence of genuinely popular cultural products. It was believed at the outset of the Enlightenment (just as it is today) that the mass of the population could not be trusted to select cultural products of appropriate quality without some form of education and direction from their cultural superiors: the advent of commercial cultural products met with calls for government standards to evaluate literature and rank authors, and for the repeal of copyright laws that led to the commercialization of artistic creations (Cowen 1998, pp. 76–7).

At first sight there would appear to be strong evidence that without some form of intervention the market will indeed produce a 'lowest common denominator' culture that panders to the public's most base desires for salacious titillation and instant gratification. The popularity of television quiz shows, soap operas, gangsta rap, hip hop, cartoons, comic books and Hollywood blockbusters, to name just a few of the most seemingly shallow and superficial contemporary cultural products, would all appear to be examples of the 'dumbing-down' that occurs when popular culture is driven by commercial imperatives.

The distinction between high and low culture that informs such judgments is not, however, an objective distinction. On the contrary, what constitutes high and low cultural products is a subjective, aesthetic judgment, given to wide variations across time and place. Indeed, it is the case that many of what are today considered classic cultural products were derided as the low art of their day: from the Impressionists who were originally excluded from the Paris Salon to the Beat writers who were at first shunned by the literary establishment, and from The Beatles who were seen the purveyors of shallow, throwaway pop songs to the abstract impressionism of Jackson Pollock that was mocked as the work of an imbecile, many of the most magnificent cultural achievements were initially derided as superficial and shallow products motivated principally by commercial rather than aesthetic considerations.

Hence, if cultural products were to be evaluated and regulated by a deliberative process – which would appear to be the logical conclusion of many of the cultural critiques of the market – many of the cultural products that are today considered classics would have received damning judgments from the cultural police. The consequence would be a culture characterized by stasis and conservatism: just as democratic control of land-use planning has led to architectural blandness in most British towns and cities, it is hard to believe that most innovative artistic movements could secure majority (or even sizeable minority) approval.

Scitovsky (1992) is probably correct to say that the appreciation of many cultural products requires an initial investment of time, but he is wrong to suggest that the market cannot meet or operates counter to this requirement. On the contrary, the prosperity created by the market has led to an expansion of education and leisure that has provided people with more time and opportunity to enjoy cultural products. The development of cheap commercial air travel has opened up the natural wonders and art treasures of the world to people whose grandparents could never have imagined such opportunities. The size of the global market for cultural products has facilitated the development of a myriad of niche markets in which audiences are able to develop the high level of sophistication necessary to appreciate and therefore to stimulate the production of high quality art. Just as a large city is able to sustain a more diverse range of cultural entertainments than a small town, so a global marketplace is able to support a more diverse range of cultural products than a less developed market. As Cowen (2002, p. 103) has described, 'the quality and sophistication of modern taste staggers the imagination', and much of that quality and sophistication can be seen in commercial settings: 'The diverse information available in a modern book or CD superstore would not have been imaginable a century ago.'

Of course, the market has also produced a multiplicity of 'dumbed-down' television formats, fast food restaurants, telephone sex lines and so forth. The availability of a large number of different cultural products has meant that many people act as undiscerning cultural tourists, patronizing and thereby supporting producers of low quality products. Indeed, many of the cultural products that aim to appeal to a broad, international audience, such as Hollywood action movies and Bollywood musicals, have a tendency to simplicity and blandness in order to transcend cultural and linguistic boundaries (Cowen 2002, pp. 102–5). It is probably fair to say, then, that the market has produced 'cultural horrors and cultural wonders at the same time' (Cowen 2002, p. 103).

The market produces both high and low culture because there is a demand for both and one cannot exist without the other. A vibrant artistic culture can only come about via polycentric experimentation and creative innovation, processes that will inevitably result in the production of cultural goods of varying quality. It is not possible for a society to cherry-pick only the highest forms of art (assuming agreement could be reached as to what constituted high art) because free creativity implies the production of all kinds of cultural goods. The reach of the market means both high and low cultural products are now more visible and more accessible than ever before, but while we may wish to eradicate cultural products that do not meet our own aesthetic standards, to do so would destroy the very process of creative discovery that the development of high quality cultural products depends upon.

The cultural impact of globalization is similarly part of a process of creative discovery that provides individuals with choice from an ever-increasing array of cultural products. A person living in London at the outset of the twenty-first century can eat croissants and coffee for breakfast, sushi for lunch and Indian cuisine for dinner. They can buy a CD of reggae music, visit an art gallery specializing in traditional African wood carving and go to a night-club that plays only Russian language music. Such a diversity of alternatives would simply not have been available fifty years ago.

A consequence of this process is that what was once exotic is now familiar. When a Londoner visits Japan, India or the Caribbean he or she will be familiar with many of the cultural products he or she will come into contact with. Similarly, he or she will find many cultural products of Western origin in these supposedly exotic countries. As Cowen (2002, pp. 128–32) has described, the cultural impact of global trade reduces diversity between countries but increases diversity within countries. Consequently globalization increases rather than reduces the possible cultural alternatives available to each individual.

When cultures no longer exist and develop in isolation there is inevitably a reduction in the cultural 'purity' of individual societies: pygmies who may have lived in the Brazilian rainforests for thousands of years without contact with the outside world may be suddenly exposed to pop music and blue jeans; tribes of Saharan nomads whose lifestyle may have been unchanged for centuries may find digital watches and off-road vehicles useful additions to their way of life.

Some may consider such seeming homogenization of cultures to be pernicious, but it can only take place if the individuals concerned choose the same cultural products. As Cowen (2002, p. 129) has described: 'The freedom to be different also means the freedom to sometimes choose the same things.' Large multi-national enterprises from Western Europe and North America that operate in the developing world may possess far greater resources that their indigenous competitors – as a result of the success of the economic model adopted by their home countries – but their brands can only become successful in the developing world if individuals freely choose them.

The international popularity of brands such as Nike, Coca-Cola and McDonald's does not provide irrefutable evidence of the successful duping of large numbers of people via advertising, but demonstrates the merits of these international products in comparison to the local alternatives.

Globalization is, of course, a two-way process. While one may indeed find McDonald's restaurants and bottles of Coca-Cola in Moscow, Java and Cairo, it is also the case that one finds Indian restaurants and Turkish barbers in New York, Paris and Stockholm. Global trade exposes people to a diverse array of cultural products and by so doing breaks down the barriers between people from different cultural backgrounds. As will be discussed in more detail in the following chapter, trade between nations can thereby have a civilizing effect by exposing people to persons, experiences and ways of life that they would not otherwise have encountered.

The cultural milieu generated by the market is not a superficial, 'lowest common denominator' culture. The claim that the market creates a debased, shallow culture where nothing matters other than material rewards and immediate gratification is not borne out by the empirical evidence. The polycentric discovery implicit in a market process implies the creation of a wide variety of cultural products, while the increased wealth that the market generates, and the increased education and leisure time that this wealth makes possible, also fuel artistic creation and appreciation.

Conclusion

The market is an institutional context in which individual choices are necessarily mediated by the choices and values of others. In the marketplace people are able to realize their own ends to the extent that they are able to dovetail those ends with the ends of others. Furthermore, choices made in the marketplace are made in the light of the opportunity costs of alternative uses of finite resources. Of course, 'individuals can be and are mistaken about what is most conducive to their own good' (Buchanan 1985, p. 27), but no conclusions follow from this: individuals may pursue ends incongruent with their own well-being in any institutional context, market or non-market.

This chapter has set out the positive contribution to human well-being made by the economic growth and prosperity generated by a market economy. The material prosperity that results from the efficiency gains achieved by a market economy brings access to a vast array of goods and services, as well as better education, healthcare and increased leisure time. The needs that the market meets arise as a result of a social process of inter-subjective learning through which consumers and producers redraw and revise their plans and their preferences in the light of the plans and preferences of others. It is only via such a process that outcomes can be achieved that reflect the relative and sometimes contradictory values and needs of a myriad of dispersed individuals. Market processes do not create a cultural wasteland in which all that has high aesthetic value is liable to be sacrificed in the name of profit. On the contrary, market mechanisms reflect and communicate individual preferences for the enjoyment of a wide array of sophisticated (and unsophisticated) cultural products.

This is not to say that the market is a utopia in which every individual lives a life of unadulterated pleasure. Of course individuals must still labour to produce the goods and services that they and others enjoy, while the fact of scarcity means that not all needs and preferences can be satisfied, but trade-offs must be made between competing needs and preferences. Global trade may bring people into contact with alien cultures and ways of life that may appear to threaten long-established ways of doing things. Over time, however, the gains in well-being produced by the free operation of markets are universal and indisputable. The market, and the economic growth it generates, empowers people to make their own choices, and provides access to better healthcare, better education, more leisure, more satisfying and interesting work, and an unprecedented array of cultural products.

The penultimate chapter of this book will now consider the argument that the market is a 'self-devouring' mechanism that undermines the 'moral capital' essential to its own long-term operation.

Notes

1. West (1969) and Lamb (1973) have compared Smith's writings on the negative effects of the division of labour with Marx's theory of alienation.

The crucial difference is that whereas for Marx alienation arose as a result of economic relationships within capitalist society and the fact that workers had to sell their labour to the capitalists, for Smith the alienating effects of repetitious work were independent of the relationship within which labour was brought and sold. Muller (2002, Chapter 3) provides a full discussion of the ambiguities of Smith's view of commercial society.

2. It should be noted that Sagoff's methodology is far from 'scientific'. It does not require a huge leap of imagination to envisage ways in which the results may have been compromised by Sagoff's and/or his students' prejudices and expectations.

7
Morality and Commerce

This chapter will consider the argument that the workings of market mechanisms undermine the very social institutions upon which the market itself depends. The successful operation of the market requires trust between market participants, and respect for private property and the rule of law, but it is argued that an externality of the operation of market forces is the erosion of such trust and respect. Hence, the market is alleged to be a 'self-devouring' mechanism that is unsustainable unless its scope is limited to ensure it does not devour its own foundations:

> [I]n order to work effectively the market requires certain moral attitudes on the part of those involved, and...there is some danger of these moral underpinnings being disturbed by markets themselves, thereby striking at the roots of their own effectiveness and efficiency. (Plant 1999, p. 10)

Or, as another scholar has put it:

> There are some reasons to believe that the dynamics of a free market society tend to erode the moral basis of our public institutions (including the moral basis of the market itself), and to undermine the personal ties that hold together family, friendships, and the wider range of associations that include service groups, bridge clubs, and the like. (Shaw B. 1997, p. 36)

An unfettered free market, it is argued, is liable to destroy those personal relationships, institutions of civil society and shared values founded upon a common life that the market itself ultimately depends upon. Accordingly, the market has been contrasted with those institutions of civil society that create and sustain the moral fabric. Indeed, it has been argued that a distinction should be made between a non-market economy that is 'embedded' within civil society and a market economy that is 'disembedded', or between 'the moral economy' and 'the market economy' (for example, Booth 1994).

To prevent the market from colonizing civil society and undermining its own foundations it is argued that a market economy must be treated as a 'bounded zone', limited to only those goods and services that are appropriately traded in the marketplace, but not permitted to contaminate other aspects of social life (for example, Anderson 1990; Walzer 1983, Chapter 4).

This argument has taken on a new resonance in recent decades because the ending of the Keynesian post-war consensus in liberal democracies and the collapse of Communism in Russia and Eastern Europe are said to have led to a releasing of unfettered market forces free from the restraints imposed by many traditional mediating institutions, such as interventionist states and powerful trade unions. It is argued that – paradoxically – the success of governments inspired by the ideas of the New Right in rolling back the state in the 1980s and 1990s have ultimately threatened the stability and longevity of the dynamic market economy they sought to encourage because a market economy without moral and social constraints is unsustainable in the long term.

This chapter will show that this critique of the market as a self-devouring mechanism is based upon a series of fundamental misconceptions about what constitutes a market economy, how markets work, the incentives faced by market participants and the social impact of the market. It will be shown that a market economy does not constitute millions of atomized individuals producing and consuming in isolation, but in reality is populated by individuals working together in firms, many of which will enjoy cooperative relationships as suppliers and subcontractors. The incentives within the market encourage people to behave with probity and honesty and many market institutions, such as brand names and guarantees, have developed which regulate behaviour in anonymous or non-repeated exchanges. It will be argued that the market is one of a number of social institutions that actively contributes to the creation of a strong moral fabric.

Plan of the chapter

The chapter will first present the critique of the market as corrosive of society's moral fabric. In a critique that looks back to the decline of feudalism and the advent of capitalism, it is argued that the operation of unfettered market forces will undermine the traditional social structures and common life needed to mediate the social impact of the market. In place of these traditional sources of moral capital, the market rewards and encourages the pursuit of individual self-interest and a value-subjectivism where the only moral worth attributable to any good or practice is the pecuniary value it can command in the marketplace.

In response to this critique this chapter will then set out the positive case for the market as a 'school for virtue', where almost all individuals in a market economy work together in firms, and material success is dependent upon the ability to meet the needs of others combined with a reputation for probity and trustworthiness. In addition, it will be shown that a number of economic institutions have spontaneously developed in the marketplace to provide trust and assurance in non-repeated exchanges. Finally, the chapter will show that the market is not a moral-free zone, but a forum within which individuals learn about the choices and values of others. Because morality is not imposed or society from the top-down by an overarching authority, but develops spontaneously from the bottom-up, the market can be said to be one of a number of social institutions that positively creates society's moral fabric.

The 'self-devouring' market economy

The successful operation of a market economy requires the existence of trust among market participants, and respect for private property and the rule of law. If market participants do not trust each other to honour the contracts they enter into, do not respect one another's property, and are not protected by the rule of law, then market exchanges cannot take place. These phenomena may therefore be said to constitute the 'moral capital' that is as important to economic prosperity as physical and human capital; there is robust empirical evidence to show that low levels of moral capital will hinder economic growth just as surely as low levels of physical and human capital (Beugelsdijk, Groot and Schaik 2004; Knack and Keefer 1997; Ratnapala 2003; Zak and Knack 2001).

Critics of the market, however, allege that this moral capital can only be generated outside the market and that market transactions consume but cannot create or replenish moral capital. Moreover, an externality of the operation of the market is said to be the undermining of those sources of society's moral capital. For these reasons, the market is said to have 'self-devouring' qualities: its operation is said to undermine its own future existence. Critics of the market have alleged that this process takes place in a number of specific ways.

The erosion of traditional values and institutions

Critiques of the market as corrosive of society's moral capital tend to start with the claim that the market undermines the long-standing social structures and shared values that have been the traditional source of society's moral fabric. In the words of Hirsch (1976, p. 117), the market depends upon a 'social morality' that is 'a legacy of the precapitalist and preindustrial past' and 'has diminished with time and with the corrosive contact of the active capitalist values – and more generally with the greater anonymity and greater mobility of industrial society'.

This view of the social impact of the market is probably the oldest ethical critique of the market, dating back to the decline of feudalism and the advent of modern commercial society (Muller 2002). Such a view is present in Marx's depiction of capitalism as a malevolent force that destroyed all pre-existing social institutions, including the social structures of feudalism, the family, and traditional and religious sources of morality, thereby plunging society into a moral abyss (for example, Marx and Engels 1985). Similar dichotomies between pre-capitalist and capitalist society can be found in the nineteenth-century German sociologist Ferdinand Tönnies' (1955) distinction between the *gemeinschaft* or 'community' that pre-dated the market and the *gesellschaft* or 'society' (sometimes translated as 'association') that was created by industrial capitalism, and in Karl Polanyi's (1944) hugely influential account of the intrinsic difference between the meaningful, socially regulated exchanges that took place prior to (what Polanyi described as) the creation of the market and the atomized, 'disembedded' exchanges that took place within a market economy.

While it cannot be disputed that the processes of industrialization and urbanization that corresponded with the development of the first advanced market economies had an enormous social impact that was not wholly benign, there are nevertheless a number of difficulties with a wholly negative description of the moral and social impact of the transition from feudalism to capitalism.

First, it is hard to share the nostalgia for feudal society evident in the work of Marx, Tönnies and Polanyi. Rather, the decline of traditional feudal structures and the customs and norms that they supported may be viewed as a positive social and moral good that has enabled people to choose their own destinies more freely than ever before. Whereas in pre-capitalist society one's place in life was largely determined at birth, today there are far greater opportunities for every member of society to achieve material and personal advancement. The decline of rigid social structures as a result of the growth and development of markets has granted people opportunities that were denied to their ancestors for generations. In particular, the decline of hierarchical and frequently patriarchal societies has liberated women to participate in society on a more equal basis.

Second, it is empirically not the case that the rise of capitalism coincided with the decline of the organizations and associations of civil society and the shared norms, values and common life that those institutions helped to sustain. On the contrary, in the UK civic associations and organizations such as friendly societies, trade unions, cooperative societies, even football and rugby clubs, all flourished in the nineteenth century – precisely as feudalism declined – and endured with varying degrees of success into the twentieth and twenty-first centuries (Hall 1999). Similarly, in the US the capitalist era has seen long periods when civil society was demonstrably vibrant, contrary to the pessimistic depiction outlined above (Putnam 2000, p. 282).

Nevertheless, the argument that the market corrodes traditional values and social structures essential to the generation of moral capital has gained renewed force in recent decades when it has been argued that the 'market fundamentalism' of New Right thought and practice has undermined non-market institutions to a hitherto unprecedented degree. John Gray, a one-time advocate of market liberalism who has now abandoned this position in favour of a cultural and environmental conservatism, has argued that because the New Right variant of market liberalism 'conceived market institutions as free-standing entities... rather than as legal artefacts, sustained by cultural traditions and sheltered by governments' it failed to appreciate the importance of such cultural traditions and public authorities in protecting and sustaining a market economy (Gray 1993, p. xii).

Whereas in the past market economies had been set within the context of a regulatory state that preserved the institutions and associations of civil society and ameliorated the more extreme social side-effects of the operation of market forces, it is claimed that during the 1980s and 1990s a number of liberal democracies (notably the US, UK and New Zealand) removed such barriers and allowed the market to operate free from restraint.

In the UK, it is claimed that the Thatcherite project of creating an unfettered market economy free from the shackles of the corporate state emasculated the principal mediating institutions of trade unions, local government and the civil service that had previously protected civil society from the full impact of market forces. In particular, the freeing of market forces combined with the reduction of trade union power led to a decline in the professions that had once provided a secure social and cultural framework for the working lives of the great majority of the population. Power was transferred from these mediating institutions to the central state which used its new power to impose market mechanisms on society as never before. According to Gray (1998, p. 28): 'The diverse institutions of governance through which power had long been dispersed in Britain were centralized in the state as never before in peacetime history. Market mechanisms, or simulacra of markets, were imposed on all of them.'

The release of unfettered market forces believed to have occurred during the 1980s and 1990s is said to have eroded the social institutions responsible for generating the cooperative and altruistic sentiments essential to the preservation of society's moral fabric. The disruption of traditional working practices and sources of employment created social instability and increased geographical and social mobility.

While these changes did bring some benefits to those individuals able to grasp new opportunities and achieve greater personal freedom, it is claimed they also undermined traditional communities and people's feelings of attachment to a particular place, hence diminishing their sense of responsibility to the other people living within the same locality (Plant 1999; Ware 1990).

The freeing of market forces is also said to have undermined the religious basis of society that was traditionally an important source of common life and shared values. Exposure to market forces is said to weaken traditional religious sources of moral authority by reducing spiritualism to little more than a lifestyle choice between the 'competing brands' of, say, Catholicism and astrology, or Buddhism and Islam. According to the Chief Rabbi of the United Kingdom, the market is 'a highly anti-traditional force... [that] encourages a view of human life as a series of consumer choices rather than as a set of inherited ways of doing things', and, 'In the process, religion itself is transformed from salvation to a branch of the leisure industry' (Sacks 1999, pp. 12–3). Whereas religion was once a means of communicating and regulating centuries-old traditions and practices that served to bind people together in communities, the commercialization of society is claimed to have reduced religion to little more than personal choice between competing value-systems that can be selected or rejected with little more reflection than that required before switching Internet service providers (see also Griffiths 1989).

Finally, the institutions of marriage and the family are said to have been undermined by the freeing of market forces. According to Gray (1998, p. 29), 'The fragility and decline of the traditional family increased during the Thatcherite period.' The proportion of women who were married fell, while the numbers of divorces, births outside marriage and co-habiting couples all rose. These changes in family structure during the 1980s and 1990s are alleged to have been directly caused by labour market deregulation that increased part-time and contract work, leading more women to leave the home to enter the labour market. Gray (1998, pp. 29–30) notes that, 'In those British cities in which Thatcherite policies of labour market deregulation were most successful in lowering rates of unemployment, rates of divorce and family breakdown were correspondingly highest.'

More generally, the spread of marriage contracts and pre-nuptial agreements are said to be indicative of the decline of marriage as an

institution founded upon love and mutual respect and its transformation into a contract like any other entered into in the marketplace.
It has also been argued that where the logic of the marketplace is
applied to the family, men will only participate in child-rearing if it
suits their self-interest to do so, leading to more absent fathers and
hence the decline of the family as the basic unit of socialization and
social cohesion (Anderson 1990; Plant 1999).

The decline of these traditional social institutions and the common
life and shared values that they supported is said to create a society
in which most social relationships are entered into only as a matter
of economic expediency between people who have little in common
with one another and experience only fleeting social contact. Such
relationships are too shallow to form the basis of a healthy civil
society, leading to a vicious circle of ever-declining moral capital and
evermore superficial social relationships.

Self-interest, subjectivism and the market

It is claimed that because the market is an institutional framework
that encourages and rewards the competitive pursuit of individual
self-interest, the vacuum left by the decline of traditional values will
be filled by the widespread adoption of a utilitarian calculus,
whereby each individual acts according to a rational assessment of
the likely personal costs and benefits of different courses of action.

Where individuals act on the basis of such a utilitarian calculus it
is believed that self-interest will crowd-out altruism because altruism
is thought to impose material costs on an individual or firm whereas
self-interest produces pecuniary benefits. Hence, it is claimed to be in
the self-interest of a self-employed lorry driver to fly-tip dangerous
waste near a school playground in order to avoid the payment of a
disposal fee at a refuse site (Page 1996, p. 15), or in the self-interest of
a business not to pay to train potential employees with disabilities or
to keep on employees during an economic downturn if its competitors
do not make similar outlays (Shaw, P. 1999, pp. 27–8). In a market
economy, it is claimed that 'the cost of moral scruples . . . is likely to
be business extinction' (Shaw, P. 1999, p. 28).

Moral or pro-social behaviour is therefore understood to have
many of the properties of a public good; private individuals will tend
to under-invest in it because the benefits that accrue are dispersed

throughout society, only appear over a long period of time and are non-excludable (leading to free-rider problems), whereas the costs are far more personal and immediate. In a commercial society an individual may judge that the costs of volunteering for a neighbour-hood security scheme, for example, outweigh the benefits and therefore decide not to participate, or they may calculate that the costs of voting (not only the time required to actually cast a ballot, but also the time needed to become informed about the different candidates and their policies) are greater than the benefits and there-fore decide to abstain from the political process.

The result, according to Coleman (1988, pp. 117–8), is that where people rationally choose between self-interest and altruism, there is likely to be 'an imbalance in the relative investment in organizations that produce private goods for a market and those associations and relationships in which the benefits are not captured [by those who have created them]'. It is claimed, then, that the introduction of market mechanisms to areas of society traditionally outside its scope leads to the spread of self-interest that will ultimately undermine the activities and informal associations that generate the moral capital upon which the market itself depends.

This moral free-for-all is said to be further exacerbated by the fact that in the marketplace what goods and services are produced, and what value is attached to those goods and services, is determined purely by the subjective choices of individual consumers and producers. For many critics of the market, this subjectivism and pluralism – where no good has an intrinsic value other than the pecuniary value deter-mined by market transactions – is incompatible with the generation of strong moral capital. As Plant (1999, p. 18) has described:

> The more the idea takes hold that all goods are to be seen as commodities and thus a matter purely of individual value, the less compelling will be the complementary idea that we need to secure a set of common moral values independent of individual choice. We cannot assume that the extension of the sphere of commodities and individual choice will have no impact at all on general conceptions of morality.

In the marketplace, then, it is argued that no good, service or institution has any value other than that determined by economic processes and hence a boundless market is likely to corrode the idea that certain institutions, practices or customs have an intrinsic worth separate from their economic value.

The danger, according to Plant (1999, p. 10), is that 'if there is no countervailing set of moral values not based upon self-interest', then 'the moral assumptions on which the market exchange rests could, in fact, be eroded by a culture of self-interest'. The preservation of society's moral capital is said to require the existence of shared moral values that stand outside the market process and hence cannot be diluted by the narrow, self-interested choices that individuals may make in the marketplace.

While the market relies upon shared norms of trust, and respect for private property and the rule of law, for its successful operation, many thinkers have alleged that the market undermines the very values that are essential to its functioning and therefore has 'self-devouring' properties. In particular, a free market is perceived to be a powerful anti-traditional force that undermines long-standing communities, social structures and other sources of collective morality. The pursuit of self-interest within the market is thought liable to spillover into other areas of life, contaminating them with the narrow economic logic of the marketplace where action is only taken if the individual benefits exceed the individual costs. It is also believed that the value-subjectivism and value-pluralism inherent to the market undermine the basis of an objective morality essential to the creation of a strong moral fabric within a society.

The market, firms and friendship

The claim that an unfettered free market has self-devouring qualities and that the releasing of market forces in a number of liberal democracies during the 1980s and 1990s led to a diminution of society's moral capital is based upon a series of fundamental misconceptions about what constitutes a market economy, how markets work, the incentives faced by market participants and the social impact of the market.

The depiction of the market as a series of exchanges undertaken by a multitude of atomized individuals ruthlessly competing against each other in pursuit of their own self-interest implicit in these depictions of the social impact of the market bears little relation to the reality of a contemporary market economy.

A market economy is largely composed of individuals *working together within firms* that may compete with one another. As Coase (1937) famously described in his groundbreaking account of the role of the firm, within a market economy firms are created to avoid the high transaction costs that would result if all economic activities were undertaken by individuals or by families. To provide certain services 'in-house' within a firm avoids a multiplicity of transaction costs and enables the introduction of numerous economies of scale that could otherwise not be achieved. The existence of firms, then, is implied by any conception of a market economy; in an advanced economy almost all individuals employed in the private sector will work within firms of some sort.

Firms exist to take advantage of the economic opportunities they afford, but they also provide an important arena where shared values are communicated and meaningful relationships are formed. Indeed, while the role of firms in a contemporary market economy may be contrasted with the somewhat antiquated picture of commercial society depicted by Adam Smith (Barry 1998, pp. 38–40), he was nevertheless correct to describe how commercial society replaced the frequently instrumental and involuntary ties of kinship and clan with deeper friendships borne from the experience of working together:

> Among well-disposed people, the necessity or conveniency of mutual accommodation, very frequently produces a friendship not unlike that which takes place among those who are born to live in the same family. Colleagues in office, partners in trade, call one another brothers; and frequently feel towards one another as if they were really so. (Smith 1982a, pp. 223–4)

Rather than implying atomized individuals living in their own self-centred worlds, a market economy forces solitary individuals into society where bonds are formed that can be as real and as lasting as the ties that exist between family members. Moreover, the friendships formed through choice in a commercial setting may in fact be more authentic than the clan and kinship networks that existed in pre-capitalist societies (Hill and McCarthy 1999; Silver 1990).

While it is the case that in a dynamic, advanced economy people are unlikely to work in the same firms or even the same industries for their entire working lives, giving greater opportunity to learn more and varied skills and to come into contact with more and varied people, it is not the case that firms will hire and fire employees on the basis of the slightest economic fluctuation. On the contrary, one of the fundamental economic problems explored by neo-classical economics has been labour market rigidities caused by wage stickiness: the fact that wages do not respond to market signals as efficiently as might be supposed because (among other reasons) employers are frequently reluctant to lower the wages of existing employees or employ new workers willing to work for lower salaries out of loyalty to their existing workforce.

Not only will most individuals in a market economy work together within firms, but many firms will enjoy cooperative rather than competitive relationships: most firms have long-standing relationships with other firms who supply the factors of production and services necessary for their own successful operation. As Lorenz (1988) has noted, relations between firms and their subcontractors will very often be akin to a partnership based upon mutual dependency, cooperation and trust, where short-term gain will often be sacrificed for the benefits of long-term collaboration. A market economy is not made up of a multitude of isolated individuals and firms ruthlessly competing against one another, but rather it is a vast web of cooperative and mutually beneficial relationships between employers and employees, colleagues and clients, suppliers and contractors, producers and consumers (see also Schlicht 2004).

Incentives, probity and self-regulation

The critique of the market as corroder of moral capital and encourager of selfishness outlined in the first part of this chapter is founded upon a misconception of the incentives that face market participants. As noted in the Introduction, the conviction that participation in a market economy had a positive impact on people's moral bearing and behaviour – the *doux-commerce* thesis – was a commonplace of Enlightenment thought (Hirschman 1982; Muller 2002).

Adam Smith (1982b, pp. 538–9) wrote that wherever commerce was to be found, 'probity and punctuality always accompany it', so that, 'When the greater part of the people are merchants they always bring probity and punctuality into fashion, and these therefore are the principal virtues of a commercial nation.' Probity and punctuality were characteristics of commercial society because success in the marketplace depended upon a reputation for such qualities. In *The Theory of Moral Sentiments*, Smith (1982a, p. 181) described how the 'poor man's son' who wished to attain wealth in a market economy had to put himself at the service of other people – even those he despised – in order to achieve the material success he desired. While Smith was extremely sceptical as to the actual moral value of material wealth, he nevertheless understood that its pursuit within the institutional context of a market economy produced socially benefi-cial consequences because it led people to be attentive to the needs of others and to build a reputation for honesty and good character.

In commercial society it was therefore in each individual's interest to establish a reputation for trustworthiness and probity:

> The success of [merchants and those engaged in the professions] . . . almost always depends upon the favour and good opinion of their neighbours and equals; and without a tolerably regular conduct these can very seldom be obtained. The good old proverb, there-fore, That honesty is the best policy, holds, in such situations, almost always perfectly true. In such situations, therefore, we may generally expect a considerable degree of virtue. (Smith 1982a, p. 63)

In the marketplace, honesty was the best policy because people would be unwilling to enter into contracts with an individual with a reputation for dishonesty and underhand dealing, thus preventing that person from engaging in further business. The institutional setting of a market economy led individuals who desired only their own personal advancement to behave as morally upstanding citizens.

Smith (1982a, p. 63) contended that for those who were not born into wealth, but must seek their fortune in the marketplace, 'the road to virtue and that to fortune . . . are, happily, in most cases, very nearly the same'. The Smithian invisible hand not only guided people towards prosperity, it also guided them to behave as moral and virtuous citizens.

While Smith's depiction of commercial society anticipated later work that suggested that cooperation would evolve spontaneously among actors pursing their own self-interest in repeated exchanges and games (for example, Allison 1992; Axelrod 1990), Smith's portrayal of eighteenth-century commercial society was based upon his own experience of transactions among merchants and trades-people who had direct personal knowledge of one another. Smith was less convinced, however, that market exchanges could spontan-eously produce such moral behaviour where exchanges were more anonymous or not repeated: 'Where people seldom deal with one another, we find that they are somewhat disposed to cheat, because they can gain more by a smart trick than they can lose by the injury which it does to their character' (Smith 1982b, pp. 538–9).

Such a view may raise a question as to the ability of the market to self-regulate in a contemporary context where many exchanges will be anonymous and not repeated. As described in Chapter 2, the more complex a society becomes the more ignorant its members become of one another, so that in an advanced, complex economy it is quite clearly impossible for any individual to possess personal knowledge of the reputations of even a tiny fraction of the other individuals they must engage with.

A number of economic institutions have spontaneously evolved in the marketplace to overcome the epistemological obstacles to the provision of trust and assurance in non-iterated exchanges and hence enable the market to self-regulate and self-replicate. Most consumer durables sold today come with a manufacturer's or retailer's guarantee that will enable the purchaser to return an unsatisfactory product, often years into the future, and thereby transfer the risk of losing out from the exchange in the event of the product being defective from the buyer to the seller (Akerlof 1970).

Brand names provide an assurance of product quality and also enable dissatisfied customers to retaliate by boycotting a brand. In an international marketplace, brand names are a particularly important means of ensuring that consumers without local knowledge will receive a guaranteed quality of service. An individual can visit a McDonald's restaurant in any major city of the world and be assured of a certain quality of food and cleanliness before they have had the opportunity to learn about the reputations of the local eateries. Brand names need not guarantee a minimum or basic standard, but may also guarantee a particularly high quality of service or product. The British restaurant chain, Pizza Express, for example, provides upmarket Italian food, while Rolls Royce and Aston Martin are inter-nationally known brand names that guarantee the highest quality in car design and manufacture.

As Klein (2001, p. 6) has described, unless consumers are confident that a new good or service will provide what it promises, they are unlikely to purchase it. Hence, an inventor who creates a fantastic new power tool, for example, 'has not produced a great *product* until he has created assurance'. Brand names are an effective means of providing this assurance. An inventor, then, may sell his or her product to Black and Decker, whose brand name carries the assurance necessary to successfully market the new invention. Black and Decker, therefore, 'is not only a manufacturer, distributor and advertiser, it is also a knower that grants its own seal of approval'. The success of a brand depends upon repeat purchases, perhaps by many different people rather than the same individual again and again, which require consumers to be satisfied with the products that carry its brand name. Branding is an important means by which market mechanisms enable consumers to avoid goods and services sold by unscrupulous traders; an economy without brands would be one where consumers were far more exposed to the machinations of the dishonest than a market where brand names predominate (Akerlof 1970; Klein 2000, 2001; Mosbacher 2002).

Many established stores act as 'middlemen' to guarantee the reputation of unknown third parties. As Klein (2000, 2001) has described, middlemen not only provide a convenient way of bringing consumers and producers together, they also act as a bridge of trust between the two. When an individual buys a stereo from a high street chain store, for example, the shop not only supplies choice and convenience, its reputation (built upon its brand name) also provides assurance of the quality of the goods sold. Retailers and other middlemen, then, supply the trust and assurance essential to successful market transactions.

Finally, there are a host of other reputational devices that market participants may utilize to provide information about the reputation of others. Educational and professional qualifications, for example, provide information about participants within labour markets. While the institutions that provide such certifications may be market institutions, such as private universities or professional associations, they will have a strong pecuniary incentive to ensure the reputational integrity of the certifications they issue. Consumer groups and organizations, such as the magazine *Which?*, provide reports on the reliability and quality of different goods and services and their producers. Financial institutions, such as banks and insurance companies, employ private sector organizations to investigate the reliability of potential clients. Without a good credit rating it is increasingly difficult to open a bank account, obtain insurance or to borrow the money required to purchase a house. It is not rational, therefore, to default on a payment, because even if that money cannot be cost-effectively recovered, a black mark against an individual's credit rating is likely to impose a cost that exceeds any benefit. Moreover, the financial services provided by credit cards and bank accounts are not limited to the obvious unsecured borrowing and convenient organization of one's finances; the possession of these items also communicates information to others about the reputation of the holder (Akerlof 1970; Klein 1997, 2000, 2001).

More than two centuries after the *doux-commerce* thesis originally set out the positive moral externalities that result from market exchanges, there is good reason to believe that the market will positively contribute to the supply of moral capital in an advanced economy. The success of individuals and firms in the marketplace remains highly dependent on their reputation for honesty and trustworthiness. In the marketplace, then, people not only learn about the needs of others and how to meet them, but also about the reputational pre-requisites of commercial success.

Moral behaviour is not a public good that imposes private costs on the individual who undertakes such action. Rather, the benefits of pro-social behaviour accrue to both society and to the individual. It will, for example, be in the self-interest of a business to keep on employees during an economic downturn, as it is likely to receive the benefits of a loyal workforce already possessing the specialized skills it requires when the economic climate improves. Likewise, an employer that invests in the training of employees with disabilities can expect to similarly gain a loyal and dedicated workforce. Equally, an individual who wishes to pursue a career in practically any profession must avoid activity that could result in a criminal record that would bar entry. As Maitland (1997, p. 23) has noted: 'the virtues are not (just) public goods – that is, unrequited gifts to society – but are a source of private advantage in the marketplace'.

Trust is a highly valuable commodity and for this reason it is supplied rather than undermined by the market. Adam Smith and his contemporaries understood that the need for probity and trustworthiness in the marketplace was a strong moralizing force, leading those who sought material advantage to adopt behavioural strategies that would ensure their good reputation.

The vast majority of participants within an advanced market economy do not engage in iterated face-to-face exchanges with one another, but the market has spontaneously developed a host of economic institutions that serve to provide the trust and assurance necessary to successful commercial exchange on a vast scale. The market does not erode trust, and respect for private property and the rule of law, but actively creates these positive qualities among its participants.

The market and civil society

Many critiques of the social impact of the market appear to view the market as a distinct entity from civil society. Such a view of the market and civil society as separate and dichotomous is also endemic to the academic literature on civil society and the public space (for example, Giorgi, Crowley and Ney 2001; Warleigh 2001). This view, however, represents an erroneous conception of both civil society and the market: in reality the market is part of civil society.

Civil society describes that part of society that is separate from the state. It must therefore include the private property titles that individuals trade in the marketplace and the firms that individuals create to lower the transaction costs of production and exchange. Civil society also requires respect for individuals and their property that can be realized only in a market order where private property rights are established and people are free to trade goods and services. Just as civil society is widely held to be inconceivable without freedom of speech to allow open competition in ideas, so civil society is similarly inconceivable without economic freedom to allow open competition in the provision of goods and services.

The idea that the market is a part of civil society is not particularly novel. The concept of civil society is one that can be traced back to the Ancient Greeks and the *agora* of the Athenian city-state and, as Madison (1998, pp. 130–1) has described, for the Ancient Greeks – sometimes thought to have developed an ideal-type of civil society – not only were civil society and the market indivisible, but the marketplace was also the very heart of civil society.

In Ancient Greece the *agora* was the marketplace, the commercial and discursive heart of the city, the public space where goods, services and ideas were exchanged. The *agora*, or the marketplace, was where people came together as citizens to trade in material possessions and to engage in the more ethereal exchange of ideas.

It is not the case, as Polanyi (1944) suggested, that a market economy is 'disembedded' from civil society, an economic system that is imposed upon society 'from above' by the state. On the contrary, the market is a spontaneous order that has evolved as an unintended consequence of the purposeful actions of individual men and women. Indeed, many of the practices and conventions of the market that Polanyi claimed were imposed on society by the state during the emergence of industrial capitalism had in fact arisen much earlier in the history of human civilization. The earliest known series of prices, for example, found in the Mesopotamian city of Umma, have been dated to 2044 BCE, more than three thousand years before Polanyi claimed the price system was 'invented' by the capitalist state (Hejeebu and McCloskey 1999).

The market is one of a number of institutions – including families, churches and religious organizations, schools, colleges, friendly societies and other clubs and associations – that constitute a healthy and vibrant civil society. There is no evidence that the market is corrosive of these organizations and informal associations. The claim that an unfettered free market undermines organized religion, for example, simply does not square with the empirical evidence. The United States, for example, has a higher level of regular church attendance than any other nation at a comparable level of development and has also been one of the world's least regulated market economies for many decades. If the alleged causal relationship between free markets and the decline of religious organizations was correct, one would expect to see much lower levels of church attendance in the US than countries like France, Germany or Australia where secularization has in fact been much more pronounced.

It is true that since the end of the Second World War most liberal democracies have experienced a decline in civility demonstrated by rising reported crime rates and growing prison populations. In the UK, the number of violent crime reported to the police each year has risen from less than 25,000 in 1950 to more than 325,000 fifty years later. Even after adjusting for the rise in population during that period, the figures still represent a 47-fold increase in violent crime (Bartholomew 2004, p. 15). Rather than being a consequence of the releasing of market forces, this decline of civility seems to be more closely correlated with the growth of the modern welfare state. The rise in crime which began in the early 1950s and has accelerated through the following decades can be linked to the perverse incentives, ghettoization of the poor and reliance on the state rather than self-help that has resulted from the inexorable growth of the welfare state. The decline of the friendly societies that once provided social insurance and mutual support for many millions of people in the UK, for example, can also be directly linked to the provision of universal social insurance by the state (Green 1993; for a full discussion of the social impact of the modern welfare state, see Bartholomew 2004).

Indeed, while it has been asserted that the UK and the US adopted a form of 'market fundamentalism' in the 1980s and 1990s that led to the unleashing of unfettered market forces on their unfortunate populations, in reality the state has remained a dominant feature of economic and social life in these and all other liberal democracies. As Gray (1993, p. 12) has acknowledged:

> The modern British state, like the contemporary American state, and like practically every other modern state, owns vast assets . . . At present levels of taxation and expenditure, something between a third and a half of national income is pre-empted by government. Furthermore, the modern British state, again like virtually every other modern state, operates a colossal apparatus of income transfers via progressive taxation, welfare payments, and a welter of tariffs and subsidies. As a result of its tremendous economic power, the modern British state continues to exercise an invasive influence on social life of a sort only comparable to that of the absolutist monarchies of early modern Europe.

It is hard to reconcile the claim that the state has released unfettered market forces upon society with the fact that the UK government presently spends approximately 40 per cent of GDP and appoints and oversees a host of regulatory bodies from the Office of Fair Trading to the Competition Commission, and from the Financial Services Authority to the utility regulators, to intervene in the workings of the marketplace.

Similarly, the claim that corporatism was a successful means of mediating the impact of market forces and by so doing maintaining an harmonious society is little short of incredible. In reality, just as Hayek (1944, 1960, 1980) and others predicted, corporatism fuelled social conflict as different groups competed for political favour and sought to use the political process to secure economic transfers and privileges (for example, Brittan 1975). Gray's (1998) rosy depiction of Britain's corporatist past in his most recent work appears to have been written following a serious bout of amnesia as to the decades of industrial unrest, economic mayhem and social chaos that resulted from attempts to achieve corporatist political settlements.

Markets, choice and morals

A market economy is driven by the polycentric actions of countless individual producers and consumers. Consequently, the value of different goods and services will be determined by the subjective choices that these individuals make in the marketplace not by an overarching authority that imposes a hierarchy of values upon society. It does not follow, however, that the market is therefore an ethical free-for-all in which each individual is free to devise their own moral schema without regard to the experiences, needs and values of others, or to long-established customs and practices.

On the contrary, as discussed in detail in Chapter 2, in the market-place an individual can only satisfy their needs and preferences if they can be reconciled with the needs and preferences of others. Hence, a French national visiting Saudi Arabia who desires a glass of wine with a meal will find no restaurant willing to supply this good because it contravenes the religious beliefs and local customs of their hosts. Likewise, a man who wishes to pursue a career in the financial sector but refuses to wear a suit and tie is unlikely to find a firm willing to employ him unless he conforms to the accepted dress codes of his chosen profession. Individual choices in the marketplace are not made solitarily in a moral-free zone, but are taken in a social and cultural context informed by a wide array of social institutions, including families, friendship networks, religious organizations, schools, universities and informal associations.

Morals and ethics have not been devised and imposed upon society from the top-down by political, religious or some other collective authority, but have evolved spontaneously from the bottom-up as an unintended consequence of the actions and experiences of generations of individual men and women (see, for example, Yeager 2001). The market is part of that process through which a shared morality is formed, communicated and developed; it is one forum where people learn what is considered acceptable behaviour in different contexts.

The market plays a crucial role in the process of challenge, adaptation and reinforcement through which society develops and evolves because it facilitates the simultaneous adoption of different alternatives without the need for majority approval before any single alternative is tested or adopted. Those 'daring' individuals who first sampled Indian food when it was introduced to the UK by immigrants from the Indian sub-continent in the 1950s and 1960s paved the way for a culinary revolution that has seen chicken tikka masala become one of the country's most popular dishes, and, more importantly, led a process of evolution that has transformed Britain from a mono-cultural society into a multicultural one.

This change occurred without the requirement of majority approval for each incremental step or the need for a collective authority to decree how the different cultures should combine. Indeed, social change of this nature could not take place on the basis of majority approval or on the direction of a collective authority. Rather, it must be a process of gradual and spontaneous evolution as different individuals imitate and innovate.

As Hayek (1960, p. 63) wrote, society can only advance if moral rules that 'will be observed by the majority, can be broken by individuals who feel that they have strong enough reasons to brave the censure of their fellows'. Social and cultural progress is dependent upon a set of shared norms and values that are observed by the vast majority of the population, and on the existence of moral entrepreneurs who are willing to challenge and test those rules at the margins. Social order requires, however, that the 'conscientious and courageous' individuals who 'decide to brave general opinion and to disregard a particular rule' must also prove their 'general respect for the prevailing moral rules by carefully observing the others' (Hayek 1982c, p. 171). It is only through such a process of observation of the prevailing moral rules combined with challenge at the margins that society is able to advance, so that, for example, homosexuality became socially accepted and legalized in the UK in the second half of the twentieth century.

It is not the case that strong moral capital equates with value-consensus. While there must be a consensus as to the most fundamental codes of conduct – that the rule of law must be observed and must outlaw crimes against people and property – where complete value-consensus does exist it is likely to be indicative of a society in moral decline where norms and rules are no longer exposed to challenge and therefore are unable to evolve or adapt.

Moreover, given that all contemporary liberal democracies are, to a lesser or greater extent, heterogeneous multicultural and multi-faith societies, a morality founded upon value-consensus is neither practicable nor desirable. The polycentric nature of market exchange means that it provides a framework within which people with different cultures, faiths and morals can live and work together. Indeed, an appreciation of this fact was a central component of the *doux-commerce* thesis. Voltaire (1980, p. 41), for example, in his *Letters on England*, described the London Stock Exchange of the eighteenth century as a remarkable example of the ability of the market to enable people of different faiths to live and work in harmony:

> Go into the London Stock Exchange – a more respectable place than many a court – and you will see representatives from all nations gathered together for the utility of men. Here Jew, Mohammedan and Christian deal with each other as though they were all of the same faith, and only apply the word infidel to those who go bankrupt.

Whereas the pronouncements of religious leaders very often served to emphasise the differences between people of different faiths and hence to lead to sectarianism, Voltaire observed that the market brought people together on the basis of their common interests and encouraged them to set aside their differences. Because the market did not impose one set of values upon people, those who subscribed to a plurality of different values were able to co-exist and trade together within the marketplace.

Furthermore, providing individuals with the freedom and ability to make their own choices – whether the relatively prosaic choices of different products on supermarket shelves, or more fundamental choices of alternative ways of living – has positive moral consequences. It is only by making autonomous choices that individuals are able to become fully moral beings: it is one of the great fallacies of socialism that individuals can be 'forced to be free'. To force people to behave morally has – paradoxically – a demoralizing effect, whereas to positively choose moral behaviour is enriching and reinforcing. The more individuals choose to act morally, the more such behaviour becomes part of their nature and their identity. A healthy civil society cannot be created and maintained by people accustomed to being herded like cattle, but requires the development of individuality and responsibility that can only come from the exercise of individual choice. Because the incentive structure of the market promotes virtuous behaviour, it is a forum in which people learn to make positive moral choices.

It is the case that when people become accustomed to participating in a market economy that facilitates and satisfies a huge range and diversity of choices other institutions that deny such choice and autonomy may seem disempowering and anachronistic by comparison. The decline in electoral participation in most liberal democracies in recent years has coincided with the growth and increasing sophistication of markets and it is hardly surprising that a process that allows people to cast only a single vote amongst millions in support of a single political party every four or five years will appear constraining in comparison to a process that enables people to select their own optimal bundle of goods and services at any moment of any day. The pathologies of democracy relative to the market are particularly apparent where each system attempts to satisfy people's preferences; it is where preferences are satisfied primarily via the political process – such as in healthcare, education and transport – that there are high levels of popular discontent. The solution here is not to reject democracy, but to minimize the impact of the pathologies of democratic government by reducing the role of the state in the economic sphere so that wherever possible goods and services are provided by the market.

The exposure of the pathologies of democracy by the market is in many respects a special case because of the overlap between the functions of the two institutions in the provision of goods and services. While participation in a market economy (or, for that matter, a democratic polity) where a myriad of competing alternatives are available may lead people to question those, such as religious leaders, who claim to possess the one incontrovertible, absolute truth, the market does not undermine other institutions of civil society because it performs an entirely separate and different function. On the contrary, the positive moral consequences of participation in the market described above are liable to strengthen rather than weaken the other institutions of civil society.

Conclusion

This chapter has shown that the market is a self-regulating and self-renewing institution. The successful operation of a market economy requires trust among market participants, and respect for private property and the rule of law – what might be termed the moral capital essential to market exchange – and the market naturally supplies these valuable 'commodities'. The development of a market economy has brought individuals and families out of their homes and into society where the great majority work together in firms, many of which enjoy cooperative relations as subcontractors and suppliers of different factors of production.

In the marketplace there are powerful incentives for people to behave with probity and honesty in order to earn and maintain a reputation for trustworthiness, as well as institutions – such as brand names and 'middle men' – that have developed to overcome informational problems in seemingly anonymous and non-repeated exchanges.

The market is one of a number of institutions of civil society that positively contribute to the spontaneous evolution of a society's moral fabric from the bottom-up; it is not the case that the generation of strong moral capital requires the imposition of a moral consensus from the top-down by a public authority. On the contrary, a strong moral fabric necessitates that individuals positively make moral choices rather than having 'morality' forced upon them. By contrast, there is good reason to believe that where the role of the state has expanded, for example in the provision of social insurance, it has crowded out the institutions of civil society that once undertook this and other functions and in so doing made a positive contribution to the generation of moral capital.

A society with a strong and resilient moral fabric is one in which the scope of the market is extended as far as possible so that as many people as possible have the opportunity to participate in the market and to learn the virtues of probity and honesty that the market teaches. There is, then, no distinction between a market economy and a moral economy.

8
Conclusion

This book has set out a positive ethical case for the market economy: only the market provision of goods and services and only a distribution of income and wealth determined by the market are compatible with the principle of individual self-ownership; only where prices are heuristically generated in the marketplace and different courses of action bring differential economic rewards can resources be efficiently allocated within a complex, advanced economy so that long-term prosperity can be assured, and only when individuals respond to the impersonal signals provided by the price mechanism can they meet the needs of people of whom they have no direct personal knowledge. The choices people make in the marketplace are not taken atomistically with a selfish disregard for other people, but are made in the context of the needs and preferences of others; the market provides incentives for virtuous behaviour and mechanisms that supply trust and assurance in commercial transactions that make it a self-regulating and self-replenishing economic system.

Hence, the case for limiting or regulating the market on ethical grounds or in order to preserve society's moral fabric is weak. Of course, as set out at the start of this book, given that the market is an institutional setting where people exchange property rights under the rule of law, there are natural limits to the market where private property rights do not or cannot exist, or where transactions violate the rule of law. But where legitimate property rights exist in goods and services there is no moral case for restricting the freedom of individuals and firms to voluntarily exchange those property titles. Indeed, extending the reach of property rights is the most effective means of capturing the externalities that may result from commercial transactions.

This book has argued that the prosperity that has been achieved in advanced market economies enables the provision of a guaranteed minimum income to all citizens by the state as part of the institutional framework within which the market is situated. Such a guaranteed minimum will protect all citizens from the possibility of destitution in the event of personal calamity irrespective of its cause. As noted in Chapter 4, the provision of such a minimum income – as with the provision of any form of minimal state – does involve a compromise between the principle of self-ownership and the necessity of raising finance through general taxation, but the morally objectionable nature and harmful consequences of such a measure can be limited if funds are raised via a flat rate income tax or sales tax.

An unfettered market economy offers the greatest prospect of prosperity for the world's poor. At present, as Soto (2000) has documented and as was noted in Chapter 4, the poorest people of the world live in countries without established private property rights and also frequently without the protection of the rule of law; in the absence of these fundamentals poor people are condemned to continued poverty. It is only a market economy – driven by the polycentric choices of individual producers and consumers exchanging property titles for goods and services – that can create the economic growth necessary to simultaneously lift large numbers of people out of poverty; no successful economy has ever been created by aid.

A free market economy not only holds the promise of prosperity, it also offers people an unprecedented degree of personal freedom. Only in the marketplace can each individual have the option to exit from those transactions they do not wish to participate in and by so doing pursue their own self-conceived ends. By contrast, where goods and services are provided by the state the majority have the ability to impose their choices and hence their will on the minority, and, indeed, the vagaries of political decision-making mean that organized minorities are frequently able to impose their will on the majority.

The market also offers the greatest possibility for harmonious co-existence among people and between nations. The market offers each individual a means of achieving personal advancement that also benefits other people: success in the marketplace depends upon the ability to put oneself at the service of others by responding to the price signals and profit opportunities that communicate information about other people's needs and preferences. By contrast, in the absence of the market pecuniary rewards can be attained only by political patronage or by force. At the international level, trade has the ability to break down the barriers that may exist between people from different cultures and countries, creating mutually beneficial and interdependent commercial relationships where mutually antag-onistic relationships might otherwise develop.

Given the strength of the ethical case for the market, it might be reasonably asked why this positive view of the market is not more widely held. One important reason, as outlined by Hayek (1998) in his classic essay *The Intellectuals and Socialism*, is the malign influence of 'the intellectuals' or 'second-hand dealers in ideas' – that is, the teachers, journalists, commentators, novelists and religious leaders, among others, whose interpretations of ideas and events inform most people's thinking about political and economic matters and therefore set the tone of society's cultural and political life.

Intelligent people like these individuals tend to value the application of intelligence above all else and therefore are inherently suspicious of the market because it is a spontaneous process that operates beyond the conscious control of any one individual or group of individuals. The influence of 'the intellectuals' has worked to create a cultural milieu that is deeply hostile to the market because the outcomes that the market produces are 'the results of human action but not of human design' (Hayek 1967a), do not conform to any particular pre-determined pattern or plan and will include economic inequalities that affront many intellectuals' personal taste for egalitarianism.

This scepticism and suspicion towards the market drives the continued desire to regulate and intervene in the economy rather than allow market forces to operate unhampered. At its most extreme, it has fuelled the desire to create a 'more moral' or 'more humane' alternative that has condemned so many people around the world to impoverished lives, from the citizens of the former Soviet Union and its East European satellites who had to endure half a century or more of state socialism to the poor of the Third World who are actively discouraged and prevented from adopting enterprise-based solutions to their poverty.

This book has aimed to make a modest contribution to changing the intellectual climate by setting out a positive ethical case for the market and by showing that the market offers the best prospect for the attainment of prosperous, peaceful and free societies.

Excessive regulation of and intervention in the market can only distort and stifle the positive benefits that it produces, but the market's long-term endurance is assured because wherever men and women are able to frame their own desires and pursue their own purposeful plans they will always seek to do so by freely exchanging goods and services in the marketplace. Wherever human societies have flourished, markets have also thrived, despite the myriad attempts to stamp them out. The promise of freedom, peace and prosperity offered by the market will always endure.

Bibliography

Aarstol, M. 1991, 'Coercion, Aggression and Capitalism', *Economy and Society*, 20/4: 402–10.

Acton, H. B. 1993, *The Morals of Markets and Related Essays*, D. Gordon and J. Shearmur (eds), Indianapolis: Liberty Fund.

Agell, J., Lindh, T. and Ohlsson, H. 1997, 'Growth and the Public Sector: A Critical Review Essay', *European Journal of Political Economy*, 13/1: 33–52.

Akerlof, G. A. 1970, 'The Market for "Lemons": Quality Uncertainty and the Market Mechanism', *Quarterly Journal of Economics*, 84/3: 488–500.

Alexander, L. A. and O'Driscoll, L. H. 1980, 'Stork Markets: An Analysis of "Baby-selling"', *Journal of Libertarian Studies*, 4/2: 173–96.

Allison, P. D. 1992, 'The Cultural Evolution of Beneficent Norms', *Social Forces*, 71/2: 279–301.

Anderson, E. 1990, 'The Ethical Limitations of the Market', *Economics and Philosophy*, 6: 179–205.

Andre, J. 1995, 'Blocked Exchanges: A Taxonomy', in D. Miller and M. Walzer (eds), *Pluralism, Justice and Equality*, Oxford: Oxford University Press.

Andreoni, J. 1990, 'Impure Altruism and Donations to Public Goods: A Theory of Warm-Glow Giving', *The Economic Journal*, 100: 464–77.

Arneil, B. 1996, 'The Wild Indian's Venison: Locke's Theory of Property and English Colonialism in America', *Political Studies*, 44/1: 60–74.

Ashton, T. S. 1968/1997, *The Industrial Revolution*, Oxford: Oxford University Press.

Axelrod, R. 1990, *The Evolution of Cooperation*, London: Penguin.

Barber, B. 1984, *Strong Democracy*, Berkeley: University of California Press.

Barry, N. 1979, *Hayek's Social and Economic Philosophy*, Basingstoke: Macmillan.

Barry, N. 1998, *Business Ethics*, Basingstoke: Macmillan.

Bartholomew, J. 2004, *The Welfare State We're In*, London: Heinemann.

Bartlett, B. 2000, 'The Verdict on the Minimum Wage: Guilty on all Counts', *Economic Affairs*, 20/3: 45–8.

Batson, C. D. 1987, 'Prosocial Motivation: Is It Ever Truly Altruistic?', *Advances in Experimental Social Psychology*, 20: 65–122.

Berggren, N. 1999, 'Economic Freedom and Equality: Friends or Foes?', *Public Choice*, 100: 203–23.

Berlin, I. 1969, 'Two Concepts of Liberty', in *Four Essays on Liberty*, Oxford: Oxford University Press.

Beugelsdijk, S., Groot, H. L. F. and Schaik, A. B. T. M. 2004, 'Trust and Economic Growth: A Robustness Analysis', *Oxford Economic Papers*, 56: 118–34.

Boettke, P. J. 1997, 'Where did Economics Go Wrong? Modern Economics as a Flight from Reality', *Critical Review*, 11/1: 11–64.

Boettke, P. J. 2001, *Calculation and Coordination*, London: Routledge.

Booth, W. J. 1994, 'On the Idea of the Moral Economy', *American Political Science Review*, 88/3: 653–67.

Bose, A. 1980, *Marx on Exploitation and Inequality*, Oxford: Oxford University Press.

Brittan, S. 1975, 'The Economic Contradictions of Democracy', *British Journal of Political Science*, 5/2: 129–59.

Brittan, S. 1995, *Capitalism with a Human Face*, Cheltenham: Edward Elgar.

Buchanan, A. 1985, *Ethics, Efficiency and the Market*, New Jersey: Rowman and Littlefield.

Buchanan, J. M. 1969/1999, *Cost and Choice*, Indianapolis: Liberty Fund.

Buckley, P. J. and Casson, M. 2001, 'The Moral Basis of Global Capitalism: Beyond the Eclectic Theory', *International Journal of the Economics of Business*, 8/2: 303–27.

Byrne, D. 1997, 'Social Exclusion and Capitalism', *Critical Social Policy*, 17/1: 27–51.

Callinicos, A. 2000, *Equality*, Cambridge: Polity.

Carens, J. 1981, *Equality, Moral Incentives and the Market*, Chicago: University of Chicago Press.

Carver, T. 1987, 'Marx's Political Theory of Exploitation', in A. Reeve (ed.), *Modern Theories of Exploitation*, London: Sage.

Child, J. W. 1998, 'Profit: The Concept and its Moral Features', *Social Philosophy and Policy*, 15/2: 243–82.

Choi, Y. B. 1999, 'On the Rich Getting Richer and the Poor Getting Poorer', *Kyklos*, 52: 239–58.

Christman, J. 1986, 'Can Ownership be Justified by Natural Rights?', *Philosophy and Public Affairs*, 15/2: 156–77.

Christman, J. 1991, 'Self-Ownership, Equality, and the Structure of Property Rights', *Political Theory*, 19/1: 28–46.

Coase, R. H. 1937, 'The Nature of the Firm', *Economica*, 4: 386–405.

Coase, R. H. 1976, 'Adam Smith's View of Man', *Journal of Law and Economics*, 19: 529–46.

Cohen, G. A. 1977, 'Labor, Leisure, and a Distinctive Contradiction of Advanced Capitalism', in G. Dworkin, G. Bermant and P. G. Brown (eds), *Markets and Morals*, London: Hemisphere.

Cohen, G. A. 1979, 'The Labor Theory of Value and the Concept of Exploitation', *Philosophy and Public Affairs*, 8/4: 338–60.

Cohen, G. A. 1995, *Self-Ownership, Freedom and Equality*, Cambridge: Cambridge University Press.

Cohen, G. A. 2000, *If You're an Egalitarian, How Come You're So Rich?* London: Harvard University Press.

Coleman, J. S. 1988, 'Social Capital in the Creation of Human Capital', *American Journal of Sociology*, 94: S95–120.

Conway, D. 1995, *Classical Liberalism: The Unvanquished Ideal*, Basingstoke: Macmillan.

Cowen, T. 1998, *In Praise of Commercial Culture*, Cambridge, MA: Harvard University Press.

Cowen, T. 2002, *Creative Destruction*, Princeton: Princeton University Press.

Davidson, H. J. 1976, 'Why Most Consumer Brands Fail', *Harvard Business Review*, 54/2: 117–22.

Dworkin, R. 2000, *Sovereign Virtue*, Cambridge, MA: Harvard University Press.

Edgeworth, F. Y. 1881, *Mathematical Physics: An Essay on the Application of Mathematics to the Moral Sciences*, London: C. K. Paul & Co.

Engels, F. 1844/1968, *Conditions of the Working Class in England*, London: Allen and Unwin.

Frank, R. H. 1999, *Luxury Fever*, New York: The Free Press.

Friedman, M. 1970/2002, 'The Social Responsibility of Business is to Increase Its Profits', in E. Heath (ed.), *Morality and the Market: Ethics and Virtue in the Conduct of Business*, New York: McGraw-Hill.

Friedman, M. 1976, *Price Theory*, New York: Aldine.

Galbraith, J. K. 1999, *The Affluent Society*, Revised Fifth Edition, London: Penguin.

Galbraith, J. K. 2002, 'The Importance of Being Sufficiently Equal', *Social Philosophy and Policy*, 19/1: 201–24.

Gamble, A. 1996, *Hayek: The Iron Cage of Liberty*, Cambridge: Polity Press.

Garrison, R. 1985, 'Austrian Economics as the Middle Ground: Comment on Loasby', in I. Kirzner (ed.), *Method, Process, and Austrian Economics*, Lexington, MA: Lexington Books.

Giorgi, L., Crowley, J. and Ney, S. 2001, 'Surveying the European Public Space – A Political and Research Agenda', *Innovation, The European Journal of Social Science Research*, 14/1: 73–83.

Goklany, I. 2002, 'Economic growth and human well-being', in J. Morris (ed.), *Sustainable Development: Promoting Progress or Perpetuating Poverty?* London: Profile Books.

Gray, J. 1993, *Beyond the New Right*, London: Routledge.

Gray, J. 1998, *False Dawn: The Delusions of Global Capitalism*, London: Granta.

Green, D. 1993, *Reinventing Civil Society: The Rediscovery of Welfare Without Politics*, London: Institute of Economic Affairs.

Griffiths, B. 1989, *Morality and the Marketplace: Christian alternatives to Capitalism and Socialism*, London: Hodder and Stoughton.

Grossman, S. J. 1976, 'On the Efficiency of Competitive Stock Markets Where Traders have Diverse Information', *Journal of Finance*, 31: 573–85.

Grossman, S. J. and Stiglitz, J. E. 1976, 'Information and competitive price systems', *American Economic Review*, 66: 246–53.

Grossman, S. J. and Stiglitz, J. E. 1980, 'On the Impossibility of Informationally Efficient Markets', *American Economic Review*, 70: 393–408.

Haines, M. R. 1995, 'Disease and Health through the Ages', in J. L. Simon (ed.), *The State of Humanity*, Oxford: Blackwell.

Hall, P. A. 1999, 'Social Capital in Britain', *British Journal of Political Science*, 29: 417–61.

Harris, R. and Seldon, A. 1959, *Advertising in a Free Society*, London: Institute of Economic Affairs.

Hayek, F. A. 1944, *The Road to Serfdom*, London: Routledge.

Hayek, F. A. 1948a, 'Individualism: True and False', in *Individualism and Economic Order*, Chicago: University of Chicago Press.

Hayek, F. A. 1948b, 'The Use of Knowledge in Society', in *Individualism and Economic Order*, Chicago: University of Chicago Press.

Hayek, F. A. 1948c, 'Economics and Knowledge', in *Individualism and Economic Order*, Chicago: University of Chicago Press.

Hayek, F. A. 1960, *The Constitution of Liberty*, London: Routledge.

Hayek, F. A. 1967a, 'The Results of Human Action, but not of Human Design', in *Studies in Philosophy, Politics and Economics*, London: Routledge.

Hayek, F. A. 1967b, 'The *non-sequitur* of the Dependence Effect', in *Studies in Philosophy, Politics and Economics*, London: Routledge.

Hayek, F. A. 1978, 'Competition as a Discovery Procedure', in *New Studies in Philosophy, Politics, Economics and the History of Ideas*, Chicago: University of Chicago Press.

Hayek, F. A. 1980, *1980s Unemployment and the Unions*, London: Institute of Economic Affairs.

Hayek, F. A. 1982a, *Law, Legislation and Liberty, Volume 1: Rules and Order*, London: Routledge.

Hayek, F. A. 1982b, *Law, Legislation and Liberty, Volume 2: The Mirage of Social Justice*, London: Routledge.

Hayek, F. A. 1982c, *Law, Legislation and Liberty, Volume 3: The Political Order of a Free People*, London: Routledge.

Hayek, F. A. 1982d, 'Two Pages of Fiction: The impossibility of Socialist Calculation', *Economic Affairs*, 2/3: 135–42.

Hayek, F. A. 1949/1998, *The Intellectuals and Socialism*, London: Institute of Economic Affairs.

Heath, E. (ed.) 2002, *Morality and the Market: Ethics and Virtue in the Conduct of Business*, New York: McGraw-Hill.

Hejeebu, S. and McCloskey, D. 1999, 'The Reproving of Karl Polanyi', *Critical Review*, 13/3–4: 285–314.

Henderson, D. 2004, *The Role of Business in the Modern World*, London: Institute of Economic Affairs.

Hill, K. 1995, 'The Decline of Childhood Mortality', in J. L. Simon (ed.), *The State of Humanity*, Oxford: Blackwell.

Hill, L. and McCarthy, P. 1999, 'Hume, Smith and Ferguson: Friendship in Commercial Society', *Critical Review of International Social and Political Philosophy*, 2/4: 33–49.

Hirsch, F. 1976, *Social Limits to Growth*, London: Routledge and Kegan Paul.

Hirschman, A. O. 1970, *Exit, Voice and Loyalty*, Cambridge, MA: Harvard University Press.

Hirschman, A. O. 1982, 'Rival Interpretations of Market Society: Civilizing, Destructive, or Feeble?', *Journal of Economic Literature*, 20: 1463–84.

Hobhouse, L. T. 1911/1994, *Liberalism and Other Writings*, Cambridge: Cambridge University Press.

House of Commons Work and Pensions Committee, 2004, *Child Poverty in the UK*, London: The Stationary Office.

Howarth, A. 1990, 'What's so Special about Coercion?' *Economy and Society*, 19/3: 376–89.

Howarth, A. 1992, 'Coercion Revisited, or How to Demolish a Statue', *Economy and Society*, 21/1: 75–90.

Howarth, A. 1994, *Anti-Libertarianism: Markets, Philosophy and Myth*, London: Routledge.

Howarth, C., Kenway, P., Palmer, G. and Miorelli, R. 1999, *Monitoring Poverty and Social Exclusion*, York: Joseph Rowntree Foundation.

Inglehart, R. 1996, 'The Diminishing Utility of Economic Growth: From Maximizing Security Toward Maximizing Subjective Well-Being', *Critical Review*, 10/4: 509–31.

Keat, R. 1993, 'The Moral Boundaries of the Market', in C. Crouch and D. Marquand (eds), *Ethics and Markets*, Oxford: Blackwell.

Keat, R. 2000, *Cultural Goods and the Limits of the Market*, Basingstoke: Palgrave.

Kirzner, I. 1973, *Competition and Entrepreneurship*, Chicago: University of Chicago Press.

Kirzner, I. 1992, *The Meaning of Market Process*, London: Routledge.

Kirzner, I. 2000, *The Driving Force of the Market*, London: Routledge.

Kirzner, I. 2004, 'Economic Science and the Morality of Capitalism', in D. O'Keeffe (ed.), *Economy and Virtue*, London: Institute of Economic Affairs.

Klein, D. B. 1997, 'Promise Keeping in the Great Society: A Model of Credit Information Sharing', in D. B. Klein (ed.), *Reputation*, Ann Arbor: University of Michigan Press.

Klein, D. B. 2000, *Assurance and Trust in a Great Society*, New York: Foundation for Economic Education.

Klein, D. B. 2001, 'The Demand for and Supply of Assurance', *Economic Affairs*, 21/1: 4–11.

Knack, S. and Keefer, P. 1997, 'Does Social Capital have an Economic Payoff? A Cross-Country Investigation', *The Quarterly Journal of Economics*, 112: 1251–88.

Knight, F. H. 1935/1997, *The Ethics of Competition*, London: Transaction Publishers.

Kreps, D. M. 1988, 'In Honor of Sandy Grossman, Winner of the John Bates Clark Medal', *Journal of Economic Perspectives*, 2/2: 111–35.

Lamb, R. 1973, 'Adam Smith's Concept of Alienation', *Oxford Economic Papers*, 25/2: 275–85.

Lane, R. E. 1991, *The Market Experience*, Cambridge: Cambridge University Press.

Lane, R. E. 1998, 'The Joyless Market Economy', in A. Ben-Ner and A. Putterman (eds), *Economics, Values and Organization*, Cambridge: Cambridge University Press.

Lange, O. and Taylor, F. M. 1938, 'On the Economic Theory of Socialism', in B. Lippincott (ed.), *On the Economic Theory of Socialism*, Minneapolis: University of Minneapolis Press.

Lasch, C. 1978, *The Culture of Narcissism*, New York: W. W. Norton & Co.

Lavoie, D. 1985, *Rivalry and Central Planning*, Cambridge: Cambridge University Press.

Lebergott, S. 1993, *Pursuing Happiness*, Princeton: Princeton University Press.

Locke, J. 1698/1993, *Two Treatises of Government*, Cambridge: Cambridge University Press.

Lorenz, E. H. 1988, 'Neither Friends nor Strangers: Informal Networks of Subcontracting in French Industry', in D. Gambetta (ed.), *Trust: Making and Breaking Cooperative Relations*, Oxford: Basil Blackwell.

Lyons, D. 1981, 'The New Indian Claims and Original Rights to Land', in J. Paul (ed.), *Reading Nozick*, Oxford: Basil Blackwell.

Mack, E. 2002, 'Self-ownership, Marxism and Egalitarianism. Part I: Challenges to Historical Entitlement', *Politics, Philosophy and Economics*, 1/1: 75–108.

Madison, G. 1998, *The Political Economy of Civil Society and Human Rights*, London: Routledge.

Maitland, I. 1997, 'Virtuous Markets: The Market as School of the Virtues', *Business Ethics Quarterly*, 7/1: 17–31.

Malm, H. 1989, 'Paid Surrogacy: Arguments and Responses', *Public Affairs Quarterly*, 3/2: 57–66.

Mandeville, B. 1732/1988, *The Fable of the Bees, Volume One*, F. B. Kaye (ed.), Indianapolis: Liberty Classics.

Marcuse, H. 1968, *One Dimensional Man*, London: Abacus.

Marx, K. 1872, *Critique of the Gotha Programme*, London: Electric Book Company.

Marx, K. 1849/1950, 'Wage Labour and Capital', in *Marx and Engels Selected Works*, Moscow: Foreign Languages Publishing House.

Marx, K. 1867/1976, *Capital, Volume 1*, Trans. B. Fowkes, London: Pelican.

Marx, K. and Engels, F. 1848/1985, *The Communist Manifesto*, London: Penguin Classics.

Matthews, E. 1998, 'Is Health Care a Need?', *Medicine, Health Care and Philosophy*, 1: 155–61.

McIntosh, D. 1972, 'Coercion and International Politics: A Theoretical Analysis', in J. R. Pennock and J. W. Chapman (eds), *Coercion*, Chicago/ New York: Aldine.

McMurtry, J. 1997, 'The Contradictions of Free Market Doctrine: Is There a Solution?', *Journal of Business Ethics*, 16: 645–62.

Meadowcroft, J. 2002, 'The European Democratic Deficit, The Market and the Public Space: A Classical Liberal Critique', *Innovation, the European Journal of Social Science Research*, 15/3: 181–92.

Meadowcroft, J. 2004, 'Externalities and the Proper Role of Government', *Economic Affairs*, 24/3: 17.

Meadowcroft, J. 2005, 'The Ubiquity of Self-Interest and the Democratic Fairytale', *Economic Affairs*, 25/1: 59.

Miles, M. A., Feulner, E. J. Jr. and O'Grady, M. A. 2004, *Index of Economic Freedom 2004*, Washington, DC: Heritage Foundation.

Mill, J. S. 1859/1985, *On Liberty*, London: Penguin Classics.

Miller, D. 1989, *Market, State and Community*, Oxford: Oxford University Press.

Miller, D. 2001, *Principles of Social Justice*, Cambridge, MA: Harvard University Press.

Mises, L. 1936/1981, *Socialism*, Trans. J. Kahane, Indianapolis: Liberty Fund.

Mises, L. 1927/1996, *Liberalism: The Classical Tradition*, Trans. R. Raico, New York: Foundation for Economic Education.

Montesquieu, C. L. 1749/1961, *Spirit of the Laws, Volume 2*, Paris: Garnier.

Mosbacher, M. 2002, *Marketing the Revolution*, London: The Social Affairs Unit.

Muller, J. 2002, *The Mind and the Market*, New York: Alfred Knopf.

Murphey, D. D. 1996, 'The Theories of Capitalistic Exploitation: An Examination of their Content and Validity', *The Journal of Social, Political and Economic Studies*, 21/1: 77–100.

National Statistics Office, 2004, *Living in Britain: Results from the 2002 General Household Survey*, London: Tso.

Norberg, J. 2001, *In Defence of Global Capitalism*, Trans. R. Tanner, Stockholm: Timbro.

Nozick, R. 1974, *Anarchy, State, and Utopia*, Oxford: Blackwell.

Nozick, R. 1972/1997, 'Coercion', in *Socratic Puzzles*, Cambridge, MA: Harvard University Press.

O'Driscoll, G. P. and Rizzo, M. J. 1996, *The Economics of Time and Ignorance*, Revised Second Edition, London: Routledge.

Olsaretti, S. 1998, 'Freedom, Force and Choice: Against the Rights-Based Definition of Voluntariness', *The Journal of Political Philosophy*, 6/1: 53–78.

O'Neill, J. 1998, *The Market: Ethics, Knowledge and Politics*, London: Routledge.

Otsuka, M. 2003, *Libertarianism without Inequality*, Oxford: Oxford University Press.

Page, R. M. 1996, *Altruism and the British Welfare State*, Aldershot: Ashgate.

Paine, T. 1792/1984, *Rights of Man*, London: Penguin Classics.

Pasour, E. C. 1978, 'Cost and Choice – Austrian vs. Conventional Views', *Journal of Libertarian Studies*, 2/4: 327–36.

Pennington, M. 2003a, 'Hayekian Political Economy and the Limits of Deliberative Democracy', *Political Studies*, 51/4: 722–39.

Pennington, M. 2003b, 'To What Extent and in What Ways Should Government Bodies Regulate Urban Planning? A Response to Charles C. Bohl', *Journal of Markets and Morality*, 6/1: 251–7.

Phillips, A. 1999, *Which Equalities Matter?* Cambridge: Polity.

Pissarides, C. 1980, 'British Government Popularity and Economic Performance', *The Economic Journal*, 90: 569–81.

Plant, R. 1992, 'Autonomy, Social Rights and Distributive Justice', in *The Moral Foundations of Market Institutions*, London: Institute of Economic Affairs.

Plant, R. 1999, 'The Moral Boundaries of Markets', in R. Norman (ed.), *Ethics and the Market*, Aldershot: Ashgate.

Polanyi, K. 1944, *The Great Transformation*, Boston: Beacon Press.

Postrel, V. 2003, *The Substance of Style*, New York: HarperCollins.

Preston, S. H. 1995, 'Human Mortality Throughout History and Prehistory', in J. L. Simon (ed.), *The State of Humanity*, Oxford: Blackwell.

Putnam, R. 2000, *Bowling Alone: The Collapse and Revival of American Community*, New York: Simon and Schuster.

Ratnapala, S. 2003, 'Moral Capital and Commercial Society', *The Independent Review*, 8/2: 213–33.

Rawls, J. 1977, 'The Basic Structure as Subject', *American Philosophical Quarterly*, 14: 159–65.

Rawls, J. 1999, *A Theory of Justice*, Revised Second Edition, Oxford: Oxford University Press.

Reynolds, M. 1998, 'The Impossibility of Socialist Economy, or, a Cat Cannot Swim the Atlantic Ocean', *The Quarterly Journal of Austrian Economics*, 1/2: 29–44.

Robinson, J. P. 1995, 'Trends in Free Time', in J. L. Simon (ed.), *The State of Humanity*, Oxford: Blackwell.

Roemer, J. 1982, *A General Theory of Exploitation and Class*, London: Harvard University Press.

Rorty, R. 1989, *Contingency, Irony and Solidarity*, Cambridge: Cambridge University Press.

Rothbard, M. 1991, 'The End of Socialism and the Calculation Debate Revisited', *Review of Austrian Economics*, 5/2: 51–76.

Ruskin, J. 1862/1934, *Unto this Last*, Oxford: Oxford University Press.

Ryan, C. C. 1981, 'Yours, Mine and Ours: Property Rights and Individual Liberty', in J. Paul (ed.), *Reading Nozick*, Oxford: Basil Blackwell.

Ryle, G. 1949, *The Concept of Mind*, London: Hutchinson.

Ryle, G. 1953, 'Categories', in A. Flew (ed.), *Logic and Language*, Oxford: Blackwell.

Sacks, J. 1999, *Morals and Markets*, London: Institute of Economic Affairs.

Sadurski, W. 1985, *Giving Desert Its Due*, Dordrecht, Holland: D. Reidel/Kluwer.

Sagoff, M. 1988, *The Economy of the Earth*, Cambridge: Cambridge University Press.

Sanders, D. 1999, 'Conservative Incompetence, Labour Responsibility and the Feelgood Factor: Why the Economy Failed to Save the Conservatives in 1997', *Electoral Studies*, 18: 251–70.

Satz, D. 1995, 'Markets in Women's Sexual Labor', *Ethics*, 106/1: 63–85.

Schlicht, E. 2004, 'Social Evolution, Corporate Culture, and Exploitation', *Journal of Institutional and Theoretical Economics*, 160, 232–42.

Schumpeter, J. 1943, *Capitalism, Socialism and Democracy*, London: Routledge.

Schwartz, J. 1995, 'In Defence of Exploitation', *Economics and Philosophy*, 11: 275–307.

Scitovsky, T. 1992, *The Joyless Economy*, Revised Second Edition, Oxford: Oxford University Press.

Sen, A. 1985, 'The Moral Standing of the Market', *Social Philosophy and Policy*, 2/2: 1–19.

Shaw, B. 1997, 'Sources of Virtue: The Market and the Community', *Business Ethics Quarterly*, 7/1: 33–50.

Shaw, P. 1999, 'Markets and Moral Minimalism', in R. Norman (ed.), *Ethics and the Market*, Aldershot: Ashgate.

Silver, A. 1990, 'Friendship in Commercial Society: Eighteenth Century Social Theory and Modern Sociology', *American Journal of Sociology*, 95/6: 1474–504.

Smith, A. 1766/1981, *An Inquiry into the Nature and Causes of the Wealth of Nations*, R. H. Campbell and A. Skinner (eds), Indianapolis: Liberty Fund.

Smith, A. 1759/1982a, *The Theory of Moral Sentiments*, D. D. Raphael and A. L. Macfie (eds), Indianapolis: Liberty Fund.

Smith, A. 1766/1982b, *Lectures on Jurisprudence*, R. L. Meek, D. D. Raphael and P. G. Stein (eds), Indianapolis: Liberty Fund.

Soto, H. 2000, *The Mystery of Capital*, London: Bantam Press.

Sowell, T. 1996, *Knowledge and Decisions*, Revised Second Edition, New York: Basic Books.

Steele, D. R. 1992, *From Marx to Mises*, Le Salle, Illinois: Open Court.

Steiner, H. 2002, 'How Equality Matters', *Social Philosophy and Policy*, 19/1: 342–56.

Sternberg, E. 1999, 'Review of "Profits and Morality" by Robin Cowan and Mario J. Rizzo (eds)', *Economic Affairs*, 19/1: 59.

Sternberg, E. 2000, *Just Business: Business Ethics in Action*, Oxford: Oxford University Press.

Sternberg, E. 2003, 'Review of "Business Ethics" by Norman Barry', *Economic Affairs*, 23/1: 60–1.

Sunstein, C. R. 1991, 'Preferences and Politics', *Philosophy and Public Affairs*, 20/1: 3–34.

Temkin, L. 2000, 'Equality, Priority and the Levelling Down Objection', in M. Clayton and A. Williams (eds), *The Ideal of Equality*, Basingstoke: Palgrave.

Thomsen, E. F. 1992, *Prices and Knowledge*, London: Routledge.

Tönnies, F. 1887/1955, *Gemeinschaft und Gesellschaft*, Trans. C. Loomis, London: Routledge and Kegan Paul.

Voltaire 1733/1980, *Letters on England*, Trans. L. Tancock, London: Penguin Classics.

Wachtel, P. L. 1983, *The Poverty of Affluence*, New York: The Free Press.

Walzer, M. 1983, *Spheres of Justice*, Oxford: Blackwell.

Ware, A. 1990, 'Meeting Needs through Voluntary Action: Does Market Society Corrode Altruism?', in A. Ware and R. E. Goodin (eds), *Needs and Welfare*, London: Sage.

Warleigh, A. 2001, ' "Europeanizing" Civil Society: NGOs as Agents of Political Socialization', *Journal of Common Market Studies*, 39/4: 619–39.

Warren, M. 1992, 'Democratic Theory and Self-Transformation', *American Political Science Review*, 86/1: 8–23.

Watner, C. 1983, 'Libertarians and Indians: Proprietary Justice and Aboriginal Land Rights', *Journal of Libertarian Studies*, 2/1: 147–56.

Wertheimer, A. 1992, 'Two Questions About Surrogacy and Exploitation', *Philosophy and Public Affairs*, 21/3: 211–39.

Wertheimer, A. 1996, *Exploitation*, Princeton: Princeton University Press.

West, E. G. 1969, 'The Political Economy of Alienation: Karl Marx and Adam Smith', *Oxford Economic Papers*, 21/1: 1–23.

Wilkinson, T. M. 2004, 'The Ethics and Economics of the Minimum Wage', *Economics and Philosophy*, 20: 351–74.

Wilson, J. Q. 1995, 'Capitalism and morality', *Public Interest*, 112: 42–60.

Wolff, J. 1991, *Robert Nozick: Property, Justice and the Minimal State*, Stanford: Stanford University Press.

Wood, A. E. 1995, 'Exploitation', *Social Philosophy and Policy*, 12/2: 136–58.

Yeager, L. 2001, *Ethics as Social Science*, Cheltenham: Edward Elgar.

Young, I. M. 1990, *Justice and the Politics of Difference*, Princeton: Princeton University Press.

Zak, P. J. and Knack, S. 2001, 'Trust and Growth', *The Economic Journal*, 111: 295–321.

Zimmerman, D. 1981, 'Coercive Wage Offers', *Philosophy and Public Affairs*, 10/2: 121–45.

Index

Acton, H. B., 77, 101
advertising, 115, 120
Agora, 147–8
Akerlof, George A., 144–6
altruism, 9, 13, 14, 24–32, 70, 74,
   111, 118–19, 136, 138–9
Anderson, Elizabeth, 33–4, 36, 44,
   108, 132, 138
Andre, Judith, 4, 7
Andreoni, James, 28
arbitrage, 90, 100
Aston, Martin, 144
Athenian city-state, 147–8
Axelrod, Robert, 143

Barber, Benjamin, 4, 112, 113
bargaining power
   asymmetries of, 4, 93–8, 100–3
Barry, Norman, 69, 141
Bartholomew, James, 148–9
Batson, C. Daniel, 28
Beatles, The, 125
Berlin, Isaiah, 15
Black and Decker, 145
'blocked exchanges', 7
Boettke, Peter, 22, 24, 48, 74, 122
Booth, William J., 132
Bose, Arun, 92
Branson, Richard, 105–6
Brittan, Samuel, 28, 85, 150
Buchanan, Allen, 128
Buchanan, James M., 46, 68

Callinicos, Alex, 78, 81
Carver, Terrell, 92, 93, 94
category mistakes, 36–7
Chamberlain, Wilt, 57–8, 63–4, 72–3
charity, 26–32, 82
   in crisis situations, 28–9, 30, 82–3
   'warm-glow' giving, 28

Choi, Y. B., 78–9
choice
   limits to, 10, 18, 59, 102–5,
   117
   in the marketplace, 4, 10, 13–19,
   24, 88–108, 109–29, 152–3,
   155
Christman, J., 15, 60
citizenship (and citizens), 4, 110–13,
   117–20
Coase, Ronald H., 29, 141
Coca-Cola, 128
coercion, 4, 10, 32, 88–90, 95–8,
   100–5
   see also bargaining power;
   'desperate exchanges'
Cohen, G. A., 3, 15, 59, 63–6,
   74, 93, 94, 122
Coleman, James S., 139
colonialism, 61–2
Communism, 92
   collapse of, 1, 132
comparative advantage, 21
consumerism (and consumers), 4, 11,
   110–29
   consumer associations, 145
   'ethical consumer', 119
Conway, David, 82
corporatism, 149–50
Cost-Benefit Analysis, 37, 44
Cowen, Tyler, 124, 126–7
crime, 148–9
culture, 4, 10–11, 109–29

democracy, 4, 42, 140, 156
   compared to market, 18,
   47–8, 110–14, 117–20,
   153
desert, 56, 67–70, 86
'desperate exchanges', 4, 97

distribution of income and wealth
  by the market, 3, 10, 32, 33–6,
    42–4, 52–3, 55–87, 155
  by non-market means, 15
division of labour, 20–2, 64, 98,
    110–11
Doux-commerce thesis, 5–6, 142–7, 152
Dworkin, Ronald, 74

education, 3, 11, 20, 80, 119, 121–4,
    129, 153
efficiency (economic), 9, 12, 13,
    19–24, 26–8, 31, 32, 33, 52, 72,
    77, 109, 131
  link to self-ownership, 13, 19–24
egalitarianism, 8, 15, 59, 63, 70–1,
    73–4, 76, 81, 157
  'levelling down objection', 70–1
Engels, F., 97, 134
Enlightenment, 5–6, 124
  Scottish Enlightenment, 5
entrepreneurship, 25–6, 48–9,
    74–5, 78–9, 105–7
environment, 4, 37, 44–7,
    112–13, 119
equality of opportunity, 56,
    79–80, 86
Ethics
  deontological and teleological
    criteria, 8
exit option, 14–18, 156
exploitation, 3–4, 10, 32, 88–108
  see also bargaining power;
    'desperate exchanges'
externalities, 3–5, 7, 27, 40, 110,
    112, 131, 146, 155–6

family (families), 7, 27, 80, 131,
    134, 137–8, 141, 148, 150
feudalism, 133, 134–5
football, 52, 59, 65, 135
Frank, Robert H., 4, 112
freedom, 3, 14–19, 24, 30, 127, 135,
    137, 147, 152–3, 156–8
  free society, 7, 14–15, 19, 20,
    83, 158
Friedman, Milton, 19, 42

Galbraith, J. K., 3, 56, 114, 115, 122
Gamble, Andrew, 83–4
Garrison, Roger, 49–50
Gates, Bill, 55, 67
globalization, 127–8
Gray, John, 1–2, 136–7, 149, 150
greed, 30
Grossman, S., 39–40, 48, 50

Harris, Ralph, 120
Hayek, F. A., 7, 14, 19, 22–3, 24,
    26, 27, 30, 38, 49–50, 52,
    53, 57, 58, 76–7, 83, 104,
    117, 150, 157
  price of tin example, 38, 49
  on limits to choice, 104, 117
healthcare, 3, 11, 20, 76, 91, 99,
    119, 121–4, 129, 153
  'hedonic treadmill', 110, 114–17
Henderson, David, 20, 27, 72, 122
Heritage Foundation, 19
Hirsch, Fred, 134
Hirschman, Albert O., 5, 17, 142
Hobhouse, L. T., 94, 104
homosexuality, 151
housing policy, 3
Howarth, Alan, 4, 65, 89, 96
  'reducibility thesis', 65
Hume, David, 5

industrialization, 6, 111, 135
inequality, 3, 10, 33–4, 35–6, 42–4,
    55–9, 63–7, 70–87, 88–90,
    92–8, 157

Jagger, Mick, 55, 67
justice, 10, 42, 56
  in acquisition, 58, 60–3
  procedural justice, 56, 58–9, 63, 65,
    79–80, 86
  'social justice', 3–4, 7, 10, 56, 83

Keat, Russell, 1, 34, 37–8, 115
Kirzner, Israel, 19, 24, 25, 28,
    50, 78
Klein, Daniel, 145–6
Knight, Frank H., 35, 44, 112

knowledge
  limits to, 6, 9, 22–4, 25, 27–32,
    42–54, 75, 80
  see also prices, epistemological
    function

labour theory of value, 92–3
Lane, Robert E., 109, 114, 117,
    122
Lange, Oskar, 24
Lasch, Christopher, 115
Lavoie, Don, 22
law
  evolution of, 61–2
Lebergott, Stanley, 120
liberal democracy, 1–4, 16–17, 47,
    95, 132, 140, 148–9
liberalism
  classical, 6, 16, 89, 94
libertarianism, 6, 89, 94
Locke, John, 14, 60–2
luck, 55, 68–9

McDonalds, 128, 144
McIntosh, D., 88–9, 96
Mack, Eric, 14, 64, 66, 72
McMurtry, John, 36, 44, 95
Madison, G. B., 147
Maitland, Ian, 146
Mandeville, Bernard, 12–13
Marcuse, Herbert, 116
market economy
  foundations of, 4, 7, 11, 19, 83–4,
    131–2, 155–6
  limits to, 1, 4–5, 7, 18, 37, 82,
    107–8, 132, 155–6
  moral basis of, 7, 8, 14–19,
    24–32, 57–67, 69–70, 72–4,
    75–7, 78–80, 81,98–108,
    117–29, 141–54
  moral case against, 3–5, 6, 8, 9–11,
    33–42, 60, 63–5, 67–8, 74,
    77–8, 81, 82, 88–98, 109–16,
    131–40
  'self-devouring' qualities of, 4, 11,
    129, 131, 133–40
market socialism, 24, 67–8, 75

Marx, Karl, 40, 71, 91, 129–30n,
    134, 135
Marxism, 6, 12, 90–4, 105–6
materialism, 4, 11, 110, 114–17,
    123–4, 143
  post-materialism, 122–3
Mill, John Stuart, 14
Miller, David, 3, 56, 67–8, 85,
    95, 100
minimum income guarantee, 10, 56,
    57, 82–5, 156
minimum wage legislation, 2–3,
    95, 108
Mises, Ludwig von, 25, 42, 61, 120
monopsony, 10, 90, 100–2, 107
Montesquieu, Baron de, 6
'moral capital', 11, 32, 131, 133–54
Muller, Jerry Z., 91, 130n, 134,
    142
multiculturalism, 151–2

need (needs), 6, 9, 11, 14, 15, 22–3,
    26–32, 33–8, 42–8, 52–4, 56, 80,
    86, 90–1, 98–100, 112, 118
Norberg, Johan, 20, 122
Nozick, Robert, 7, 16, 57–67, 72,
    79–80, 82, 89, 102–3, 106

Olsaretti, Serena, 96–7
O'Neill, John, 34, 39–42, 48, 50–2
Otsuka, Michael, 15

Paine, Thomas, 6
Pennington, Mark, 47, 119, 123
Philips, Anne, 60
Pizza Express, 144
Plant, Raymond, 5, 55, 131, 137, 138,
    139–40
Polanyi, Karl, 134–5, 148
Pollock, Jackson, 125
Postrel, Virginia, 121
power
  in the market, 4, 14–18, 33–4, 36,
    42–4, 63–6, 88–108
  of the state, 17–18, 66, 149
  see also bargaining power;
    purchasing power

prejudice, 29
prices
  coordinating function, 9, 13,
    19, 21–4, 33–4,
    38–42, 48–54, 67–8,
    73–5, 99
  distortions of, 27, 33–8, 42–8,
    52–3, 67–8
  epistemological function, 6, 9,
    13, 18, 21–4, 27–9,
    33–54, 67–8, 73–4, 106,
    118, 155
  objective or 'just' price, 35–6, 43–4,
    52, 91, 101
  origins of, 148
private property/property rights, 5,
  8, 11, 14–16, 60–3, 83, 131, 133,
  140, 147, 154, 155–6
  legal and historical basis of, 60–3
profits, 13–14, 23–31, 36, 73–4, 77,
  78, 90–2, 98–100
prostitution, 4, 97–8, 107
public goods, 18, 138–9, 146
public service broadcasting, 4
public spending, 3, 17, 20, 149
purchasing power, 9, 10, 33–6,
  42–4, 52–4
Putnam, Robert D., 135

Ratnapala, Suri, 90–1, 134
Rawls, John, 16, 69, 70–1, 75, 80
  difference principle, 70–1
regulation
  self-regulation by the market, 1–3,
    9, 11, 108, 142
  by the state, 1–5, 27, 78, 94, 108,
    124, 132, 136, 149, 157–8
reputation, 11, 142–7
Reynolds, Morgan O., 24
Roemer, John, 93
Rolls, Royce, 144
Rothbard, Murray, 24
rule of law, 5, 8, 11, 131, 133, 140,
  147, 154, 156
Ruskin, John, 13
Ryan, Cheyney, 60
Ryle, Gilbert, 37

Sacks, Jonathan, 137
Sadurski, Wojciech, 68–9
Sagoff, Mark, 4, 37, 44, 112–13, 130n
Sanders, David, 120
Satz, Debra, 107
Schumpeter, Joseph A., 106
Scitovsky, Tibor, 115–16, 125
Seldon, Arthur, 120
self-interest, 5, 12–13, 25–31, 46,
  111–13, 117–20, 133,
  138–40, 143, 146
selfishness, 9, 12–13, 25–31,
  70, 110
self-ownership, 7, 8, 14–19, 20–4, 60,
  82, 89, 155, 156
  defined, 14
Sen, Amartya, 82–3
Shaw, Bill, 131
Shaw, Patrick, 138
Smith, Adam, 5, 12, 20–1, 25–6, 75,
  91, 110–11, 121, 129–30n,
  141–4, 146
  'Butcher, brewer and baker' quote,
    12, 25–6, 91
  on negative moral impact of
    market, 110–11, 121
  on positive moral impact of
    market, 141–4
socialism, 1–3, 12, 24, 26, 59,
  74, 157
  endurance of, 2–3, 157
  see also egalitarianism; Marxism;
    Marx, Karl
Soto, Hernando de, 61, 156
Sowell, Thomas, 45, 73, 100, 119
Steele, David Ramsay, 24, 51–2
Steiner, Hillel, 71
Sternberg, Elaine, 8
Stiglitz, Joseph, 39–40, 48, 50
Surrogacy (commercial), 4, 97–8, 104,
  107, 108n
synoptic delusion, 51

Taliban, 121
taxation, 3, 15–19, 56, 78, 149, 156
Taylor, Fred, 24
Temkin, Larry, 71

Thomsen, Esteban F., 39, 48, 50
Tönnies, Ferdinand, 134, 135
trade unions, 132, 135, 136

urbanization, 6, 135

Van Gogh, Vincent
  Dr Gachet portrait, 35–6
Voltaire, 152

Wachtel, Paul, 114
Walzer, Michael, 4, 7, 37, 102, 132
war, 37–8, 47
Ware, Alan, 137

Warren, Mark, 113
welfare state, 20, 82–5, 149
well-being, 4, 10–11, 32, 109–29
Wertheimer, Alan, 89, 103
West, Edwin G., 129n
Wilkinson, T. M., 89, 95
Wilson, James Q., 111
Wolff, Jonathan, 16, 63
Wood, Allen W., 88, 99

Yeager, Leland, 150
Young, Iris Marion, 71

Zimmerman, David, 95, 96